GW01465166

Study Notes for Technicians
Microelectronic Systems Level 3

Other titles in the McGraw-Hill Study Notes for Technicians Series:

Pratley, J. B.: **Study Notes for Technicians** *Electrical and Electronic Principles Volume 1*

Pratley, J. B.: **Study Notes for Technicians** *Electrical and Electronic Principles Volume 2*

Pratley, J. B.: **Study Notes for Technicians** *Electrical and Electronic Principles Volume 3*

Holland, R. C.: **Study Notes for Technicians** *Microelectronic Systems Levels 1 and 2*

Study Notes for Technicians

Microelectronic Systems Level 3

R. C. Holland
West Glamorgan Institute of Higher Education

McGRAW-HILL Book Company (UK) Limited

London · New York · St Louis · San Francisco · Auckland · Bogotá
Guatemala · Hamburg · Johannesburg · Lisbon · Madrid · Mexico
Montreal · New Delhi · Panama · Paris · San Juan · São Paulo
Singapore · Sydney · Tokyo · Toronto

Published by
McGRAW-HILL Book Company (UK) Limited
MAIDENHEAD · BERKSHIRE · ENGLAND

British Library Cataloguing in Publication Data

Holland, R. C.
    Microelectronic systems level 3.—(Study notes
    series; 5)
    1. Microelectronics
    I. Title   II. Series
    621.381'71   TK7874

    ISBN 0-07-084675-8

Library of Congress Cataloging in Publication Data

Holland, R. C.
    Study notes for technicians.

    (Study notes series)
    1. Microelectronics.   I. Title.   II. Series.
    TK7874.H63   1983   621.381'7   83-757
    ISBN 0-07-084675-8

1234 PB 843

PAGE
BROS Printed in Great Britain by
      Page Bros (Norwich) Ltd

Contents

Preface   vii

1   Microcomputer Hardware   1

1.1   Microcomputer Circuitry   1
     Examples 1–3   2
     Exercises 1–16   4
1.2   Memory Read/Write Timing   5
     Examples 4–7   6
     Exercises 17–26   8

2   Input/Output   9

2.1   Input/Output Timing   9
     Examples 1–5   10
     Exercises 1–17   13
2.2   Interfacing Circuitry   14
     Examples 6–12   15
     Exercises 18–38   20

3   Subroutines and Stack   22

3.1   Subroutines   22
     Examples 1–4   22
     Exercises 1–8   23
3.2   Stack   24
     Examples 5–7   25
     Exercises 9–19   27

4   Interrupts   28

4.1   Interrupt Action   28
     Examples 1–2   29
     Exercises 1–11   30
4.2   Programming Interrupts   31
     Examples 3–5   32
     Exercises 12–21   33

5   **Microelectronic Stores**   **35**

5.1   Memory Devices   35
     Examples 1–4   35
     Exercises 1–20   37
5.2   Memory Systems   39
     Examples 5–8   41
     Exercises 21–32   43

6   **Timers**   **46**

     Examples 1–3   46
     Exercises 1–11   48

7   **Programming Examples**   **50**

     Examples 1–7   52
     Exercises 1–15   59

     Appendix   61

     Answers to Exercises   81

Preface

This book covers the syllabus of the TEC (Technician Education Council) unit titled Microelectronic Systems III; this unit covers 90 hours of study. The book is the second in a series which is designed to support the TEC levels I to V microelectronic units. However the work is intended to appeal also to a readership outside this student grouping and, if read in conjunction with the first book in the series, it should enable the reader to develop a detailed understanding of the subject of microelectronics and microcomputers. If it is read in isolation, then the reader should possess some introductory knowledge of the subject.

The format used in the text is that applied generally in the McGraw-Hill Study Note series, viz. to introduce each topic with a description of principle, followed by a series of worked examples and a selection of exercises for the student to complete. Answers are given at the end of the book. The author's choice of examples and exercises is based upon extensive practical teaching of these microelectronic subjects.

Most practical examples, including programs, are based on the Intel 8085 microprocessor. However the close similarity of this device to the Zilog Z80 microprocessor enables such examples to be transposed readily to the alternative manufacturer's equipment. It is felt that an important element of simplicity would have been lost if the text had attempted to cover different types of microprocessors. Clearly the topic of microelectronics demands practical training to augment a text of this type, and several manufacturers and distributors. (Hewlett-Packard, Intel, Multitech Microprofessor, RS Components, Texas Instruments, Rockwell, etc.) offer cheap microcomputer training boards which serve this role admirably.

The author wishes to thank his family and colleagues for their support during the preparation of this book.

Other books in this series cover levels I, II, IV and V microelectronic units.

1 Microcomputer hardware

1.1 Microcomputer circuitry

The standard three-block block diagram representation of a microcomputer is shown in Fig. 1.1.

or input/output location on the address bus and the data are transferred in or out of the CPU on the data bus. The control bus gives timed control signals to permit these transfers.

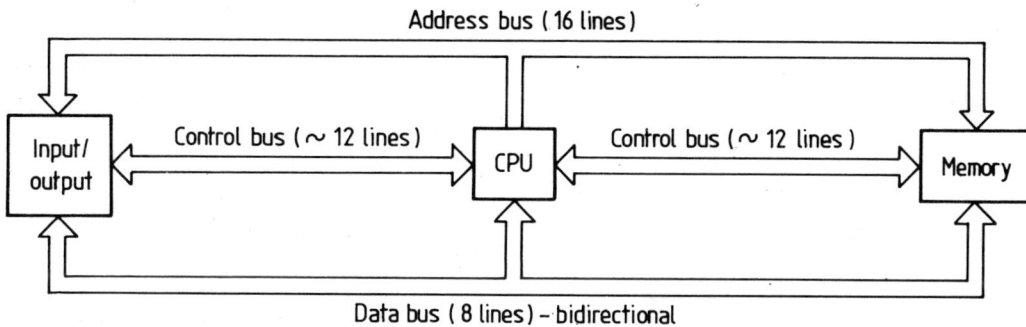

Figure 1.1   Block diagram of microcomputer

The operation of the microcomputer is controlled by the CPU (central processor unit), which is perhaps better known as the microprocessor. Normally the microprocessor is constructed on a single 40-pin IC (integrated circuit) or 'chip'. Similarly, whole memory modules and input/output circuits are assembled on single ICs.

The CPU examines the program of instructions, which are held in memory, and performs various processing operations and input/output transfers as demanded by the program.

Input/output chips drive devices such as operator keyboards, television monitors, printers, floppy disks, and remote instrumentation.

The CPU sets the address of the selected memory

This block diagram representation of a microcomputer converts to the simplified line diagram shown in Fig. 1.2 for a particular configuration. The example uses one ROM and one RAM chip and the input/output chip handles eight input and eight output signal lines.

It is not difficult to transpose this representation into a full and detailed line diagram of a complete microcomputer circuit. This is one of the principal advantages of microcomputers compared with the previous generations of minicomputers and mainframe computers. It is relatively simple to connect the modular IC building blocks together to construct a full system.

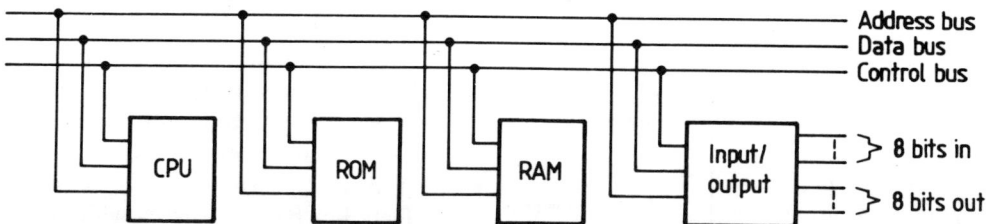

Figure 1.2   Simplified line diagram of a microcomputer

Examples

1. Draw the microcomputer circuit (or schematic) diagram for the following selection of ICs when assembled into a complete microcomputer system.

(a) CPU

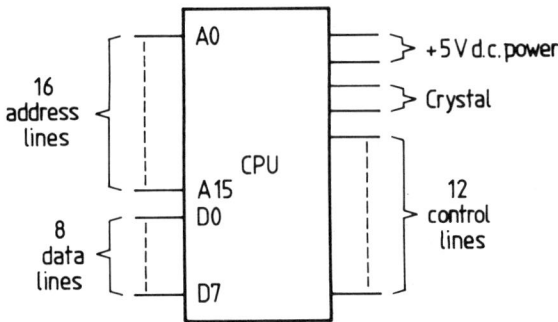

(b) ROM (2048 × 8 bits)

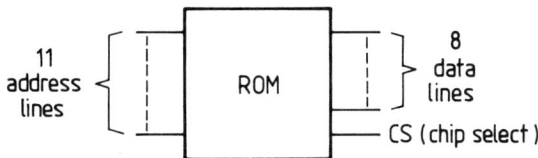

(Note: Eleven address lines give $2^{11} = 2048$ memory locations.)

(c) RAM (512 × 8 bits)

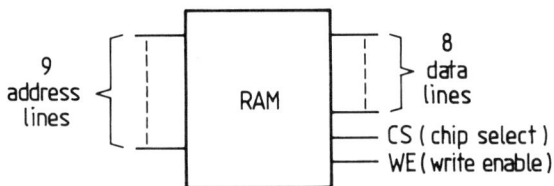

(Note: nine address lines give $2^9 = 512$ memory locations.)

(d) Input/output (eight input, eight output signals)

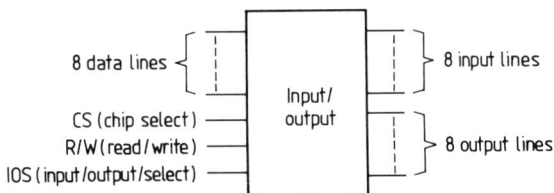

(e) Address decoder

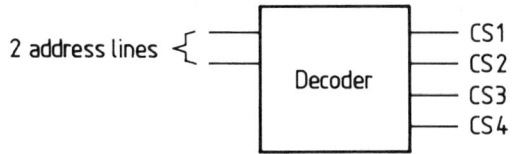

(Note: The precise function of this IC will be described later. Simply it generates a Chip Select signal for only one of the memory or input/output chips in the system at any time.)

Answer: (*see figure top of opposite page*)

Note the following points:
(a) CPU. Some microprocessors require more than one d.c. power supply (e.g., $+5$ V, -5 V, $+12$ V together with a common 0 V line). Also some microprocessors require an external multivibrator circuit associated with the crystal to produce the system clock.
(b) ROM. The least significant 11 address lines are connected.
(c) RAM. One additional signal line is necessary with RAM when compared with ROM — WE, or Write Enable. This is to activate the write rather than the read function; ROM can only be read.
(d) Input/output. R/W (read/write) is a control bus line which determines the direction of data transfer, i.e., input to CPU or output from CPU. Similarly, IOS (input/output select) distinguishes between memory and input/output.
(e) Address decoder. The most significant two address lines are used to produce a Chip/Select signal for either ROM, RAM or input/output. One of the four Chip/Select output signals is therefore not used in this system.

2. The Intel 8085 microprocessor multiplexes the data bus and one half of the address bus, i.e., they share the same eight-pin connections (they are split into the separate bus systems — 16 address lines and 8 data lines — by external circuitry). How many pins are available for control lines if a single $+5$ V power supply is required?

Answer: The following pin functions are required:
(a) Address bus   16
(b) Data bus   0 (shared with one-half of the address bus)

+5 V
0 V

Crystal

A0
A15
CPU
D0
D7
Control signals

Address bus

ROM
A0
A10
D0
D7 CS

RAM
A0
A8
D0
D7
WE CS

Input/output
D0
D7
R/W
IOS CS

8 inputs
8 outputs

Decoder
A14
A15

SPARE
ROME
RAME
IOE

Data bus

Control bus

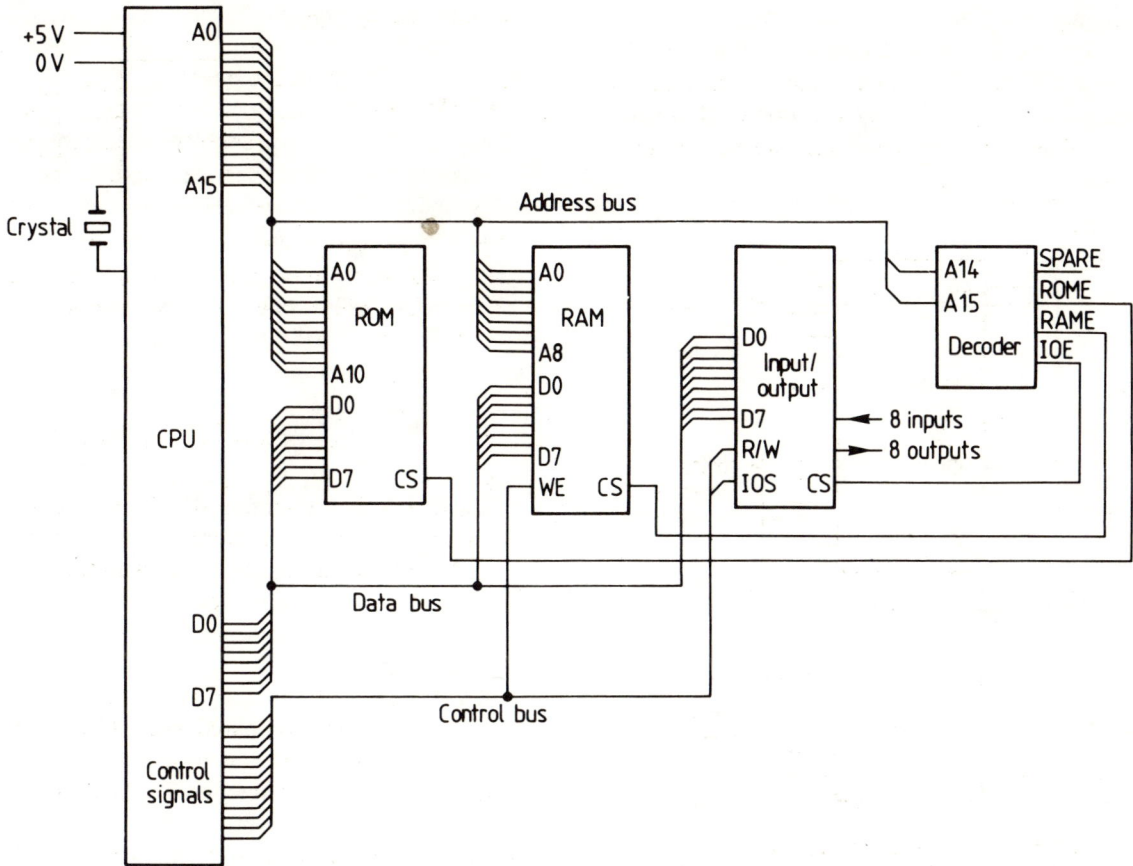

(c) D.C. power   2
(d) Crystal   2
                   ———
        Total =   20

Therefore 20 (40−20) pins are available for control lines, assuming a 40-pin package.

3. The following diagram indicates the pin layout of the Texas Instruments 16-bit 9980A microprocessor:

Answer the following:
(a) How many d.c. power supplies are required to drive the device?
(b) What is distinctive about the address bus?
(c) What is distinctive about the data bus?

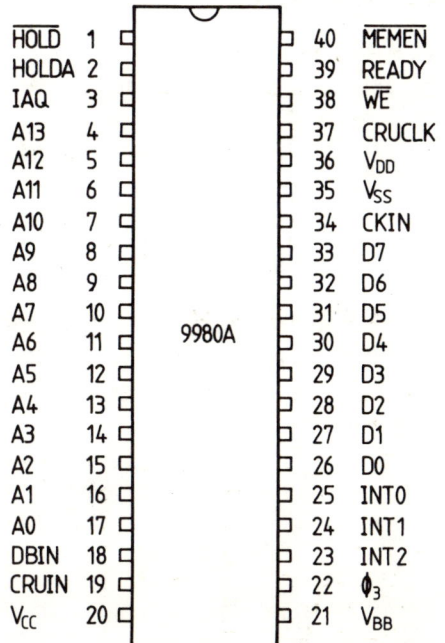

		9980A		
$\overline{HOLD}$	1		40	$\overline{MEMEN}$
HOLDA	2		39	READY
IAQ	3		38	$\overline{WE}$
A13	4		37	CRUCLK
A12	5		36	V_{DD}
A11	6		35	V_{SS}
A10	7		34	CKIN
A9	8		33	D7
A8	9		32	D6
A7	10		31	D5
A6	11		30	D4
A5	12		29	D3
A4	13		28	D2
A3	14		27	D1
A2	15		26	D0
A1	16		25	INT0
A0	17		24	INT1
DBIN	18		23	INT2
CRUIN	19		22	ϕ_3
V_{CC}	20		21	V_{BB}

(d) Why do you think that it is necessary to connect a circuit similar to the following to pin 34?

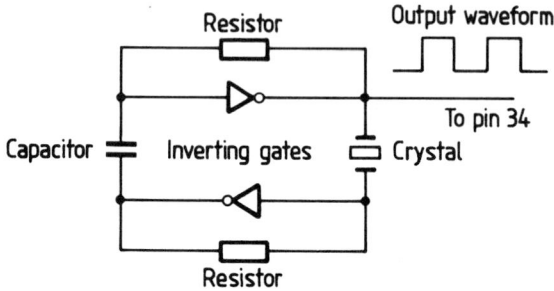

Answer:

(a) 3 (V_{CC}, V_{DD}, V_{BB}, and V_{SS} comprise three supply lines plus a common 0 V).

(b) The address bus has only 14 lines. Therefore the memory addressing range of this microprocessor is $2^{14} = 16\,384$ locations.

(c) The data bus is the normal eight-bit size. This is incompatible with a 16-bit microprocessor, which handles data in 16-bit modules. However, this is overcome by time-multiplexing two successive memory bytes during memory read/write operations.

(d) The circuit shown is a crystal-controlled multivibrator (oscillator) circuit, which generates the pulse stream for the CPU clock. Thus the oscillator circuit is 'off-chip', cf. the Intel 8085 microprocessor which requires only the crystal to be connected to the CPU.

Exercises

1. Name the three blocks in the three-block diagram of a microcomputer.

2. List four items of peripheral equipment which are often connected to microcomputers.

3. What are the 'busses'?

4. How many lines would you expect to see in the data bus for: (a) the 8-bit microprocessor, (b) the 16-bit microprocessor?

5. What function does a crystal serve in a microcomputer?

6. The 16-bit Intel 8086 microprocessor possesses 20 address lines. What is the memory addressing range of the device?

7. Locate the manufacturer's data sheets for any microprocessor other than the Intel 8085 (this is described in the Appendix) and compare its facilities with the 8085.

8. Which additional signal distinguishes a RAM IC from a ROM IC?

9. Which five different ICs would you expect to see in a minimal microcomputer configuration?

10. Which of these IC types is the following device?

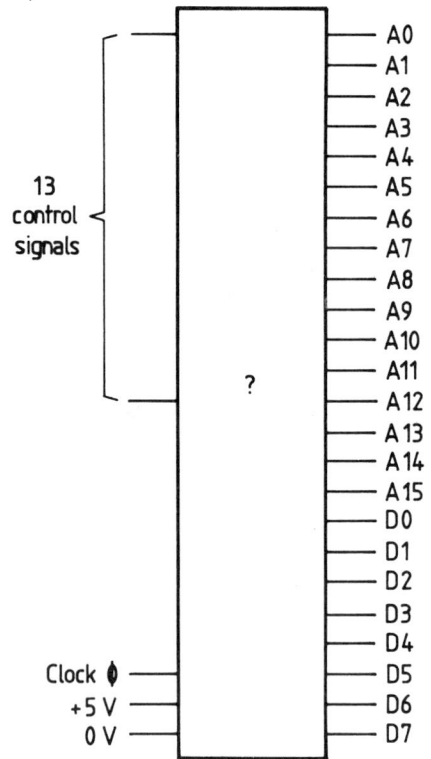

11. If a microprocessor requires the following d.c. supply pin connections:

$$+5\,V, \ -5\,V, \ +12\,V, \ 0\,V$$

how many lines are available for the control bus?

12. List the pin functions of a 1024×8 ROM chip.

13. List the pin functions of a 256×8 RAM chip.

14. Sketch the schematic diagram of the section of a microcomputer which comprises the following four ICs:
    (a) microprocessor (eight-bit, with 64K addressing range);
    (b) 256×8 ROM;
    (c) 64×8 RAM;
    (d) a 2 to 4 decoder

15. Sketch the schematic diagram of a microcomputer which possesses the following three ICs:
    (a) microprocessor (eight-bit, with 64K addressing range);
    (b) single chip which combines a 1024×8 ROM with an eight-bit input/output port (which is connected for eight output signal lines);
    (c) a 2 to 4 decoder

16. Consider the following diagram:

A7	V$_{CC}$
A6	A8
A5	A9
A4	CS2
A3	CS1
A2	A10
A1	A11
A0	D7
D0	D6
D1	D5
D2	D4
V$_{SS}$	D3

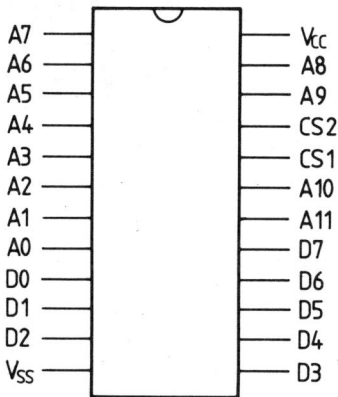

    (a) Identify the device.
    (b) Describe the pin functions.

1.2 Memory read/write timing

The microcomputer is continually performing memory read and write operations. The implementation of each instruction first involves a memory read operation to fetch the opcode from memory into the instruction register. Most instructions require further memory transfers during the execute part of the fetch/execute cycle.

The timing of the basic memory read operation is shown in Fig. 1.3. The top waveform shows that the address lines are first set and then retained for the entire duration of the operation. The crossover effect on the waveform shows that each address line may be set high or low depending upon the particular address which is selected.

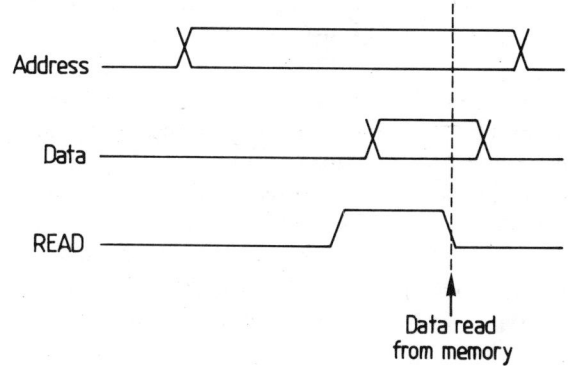

Figure 1.3 Timing diagram for memory read

The address must be stable for a time sufficient to allow the selected memory device to perform internal decoding to select the demanded memory cell, e.g., the thirteenth byte in a 128×8 ROM chip. The READ pulse then occurs, and the memory device places its data on the data bus. The data are allowed to settle before passing into the microprocessor on the falling edge of the READ pulse.

The timing for the write operation is similar and is shown in Fig. 1.4. Once again the address bus must

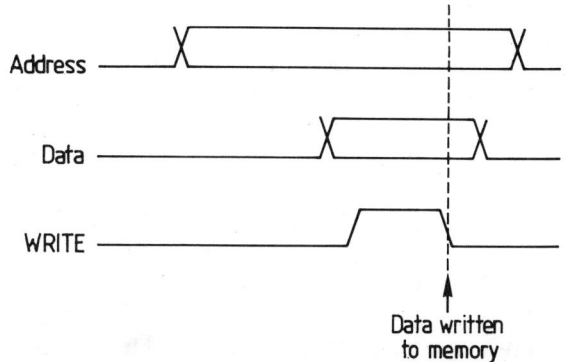

Figure 1.4 Timing diagram for memory write

be stable for a short period to allow address decoding to occur before data are placed on the data bus. The data must also be held stable for a short period before the falling edge of the WRITE pulse triggers the data to be written into the selected memory cell.

This simplified description of memory read and write operations is often complicated by the different ways in which manufacturers design for CPU and memory timing. For example, both the Intel 8085 and the Zilog Z80 microprocessors possess the READ and WRITE signals in their control busses, but very often they are not connected to memory devices if data transfer can be accomplished without them. The Motorola 6800 does not possess such control signals at all. However, an essential control signal in the case of all RAM devices is the WE (Write Enable — although often given different names by different manufacturers) signal which determines whether data are to be read from or written to memory.

Examples

4. Show the interconnections between CPU and ROM (1024×8) with the Read control signal incorporated.
Answer:

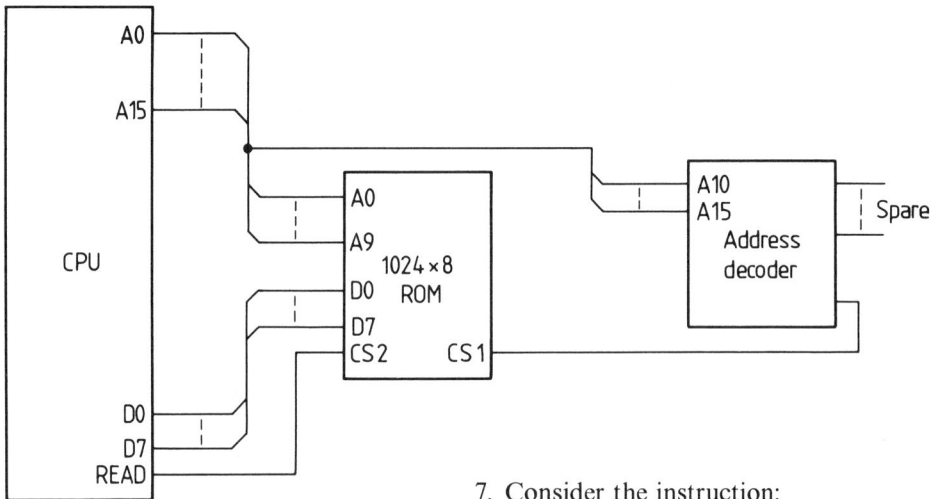

Notice that the ROM chip is activated by two Chip Select signals (CS1 and CS2), which must be set

simultaneously. CS1 is set when the address decoder IC (or circuit) selects this particular memory device rather than any other in the system. This is the block address decoding mechanism. CS2 is the READ control signal. In practice normally one Chip Select signal must be set high and the other must be set low.

5. Show that the WRITE control signal alone can be utilized to provide data transfer (in or out) control between CPU and RAM (128×8).
Answer: (see figure top of opposite page)

6. Redraw Figure 1.3 and indicate when data on the data bus are valid, invalid, and uncertain.
Answer:

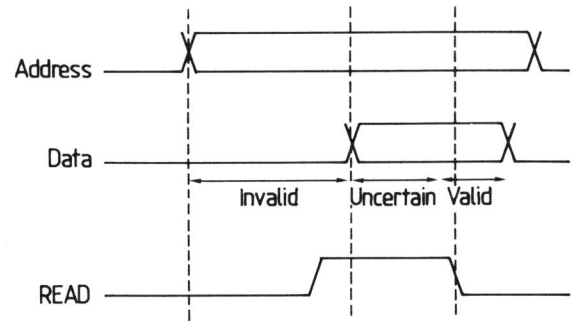

7. Consider the instruction:

STA   0B24H Store   accumulator   in   memory
location 0B24

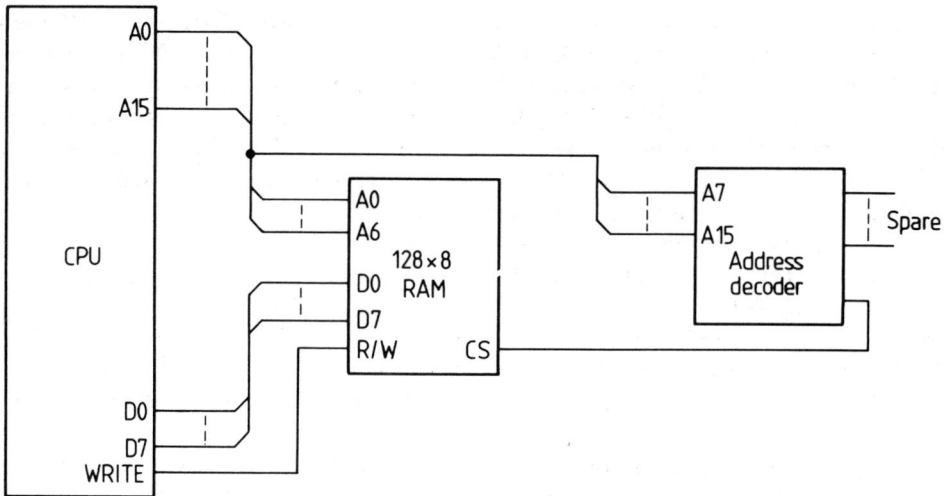

which occupies three bytes of memory as follows:
Memory location

0C10	3A	Opcode
0C11	24	Lower order byte of address
0C12	0B	Higher order byte of address

Show on a timing diagram how the basic memory read and write operations are incorporated into the fetch/execute cycle for the complete instruction. The steps which are performed are:

(a) Memory read — fetch opcode;
(b) Memory read — fetch lower order byte of memory address;
(c) Memory read — fetch higher order byte of memory address;
(d) Memory write — write accumulator contents to memory address.

Answer:

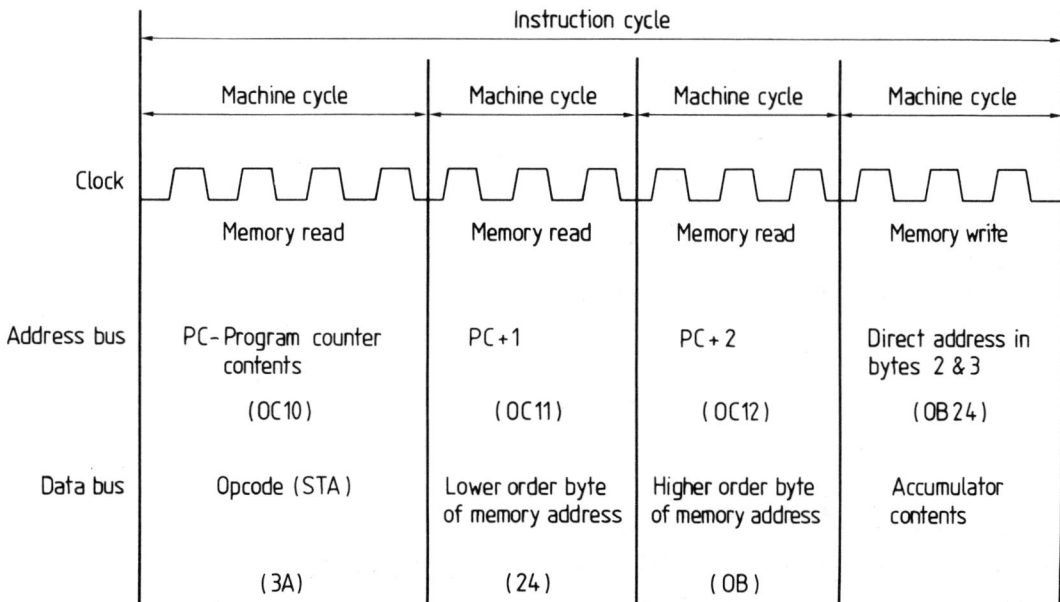

Notice:

(a) The last three 'machine cycles' follow the memory read and write timing sequences which were described previously, i.e., the address lines are set for virtually the whole of the machine cycle but the data lines are set for only part of this period.

(b) The opcode fetch machine cycle takes longer (four CPU clock pulses in place of three) than the simple memory read operation. This is because the CPU requires extra time to interpret the opcode which is read from memory.

(c) This timing diagram refers to the Intel 8085 microprocessor, although the Zilog Z80 microprocessor possesses an almost identical sequence. However, the Motorola 6800 performs a memory read or write operation for just one CPU clock pulse; thus its clock is slower than for the other devices. The clock speed is not therefore a true indication of instruction execution times when comparisons between different microprocessors are made.

Exercises

17. Each instruction involves a memory read operation. Justify this statement.

18. What is the significance of the crossover effect in the following timing waveform?

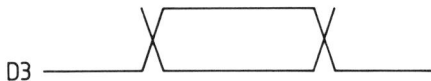

19. Some microprocessors (8085, 8086) possess on-chip oscillators with pin connections to an external crystal for precise timing control. Other microprocessors (8080, Z80, TMS 9980A) require an external oscillator circuit together with the synchronizing crystal. Which is better and why?

20. What is the approximate time difference in execution speeds for the following instructions in an eight-bit microprocessor?
  (a) Move data from one CPU register to another.
  (b) Move data from one CPU register to a memory location (defined in the second and third bytes of the instruction). Justify your answer.

21. Are the data bus lines set for longer than the address bus lines during memory read and write operations?

22. It was stated earlier that the READ and WRITE signals are not often connected to memory devices. Is that the case with the ROM IC in Sec. 1.1, Example 1?

23. Draw the interconnections between CPU and ROM (4096×8) using the READ control signal.

24. Give two reasons why the following timing diagram will not give successful data transfer between CPU and memory.

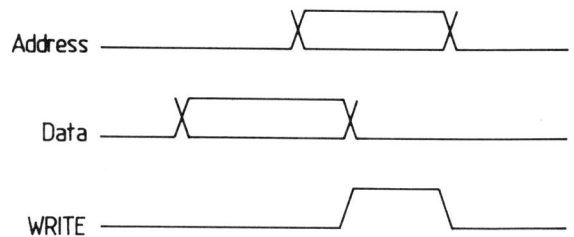

25. Sketch the interconnections between CPU and the following IC which combines 2048×8 ROM with an eight-bit input/output port.

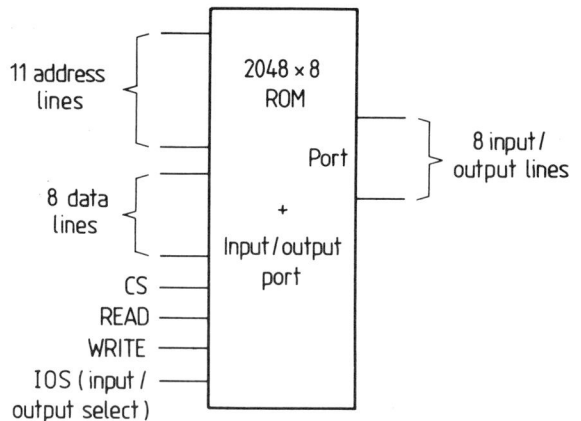

26. Examine Example 7 and draw the timing diagram for the instruction:

LDA 143CH

2 Input/Output

2.1 Input/output timing

Program execution within a microcomputer is extremely fast. Typically 200 000 instructions can be executed every second (if the average instruction time is 5 microseconds, or 5 μS — 1 μs $= 10^{-6}$ s). Input/output devices, which are often electromechanical devices, operate more slowly.

Typical response times of input/output devices are (1 ms $= 1$ millisecond $= 10^{-3}$ s):

(a) Printer: 10 ms print time for each character (100 characters/s)

(b) Floppy disk: 30 ms access time to locate required position on disk surface for read/write operations (370 rev/min rotational speed)

(c) Keyboard: variable depending upon speed of operation of operator (perhaps one key pressed every second).

Clearly a program can execute many instructions while a peripheral device, which it is controlling, is

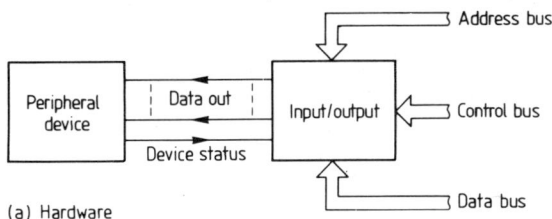

(a) Hardware

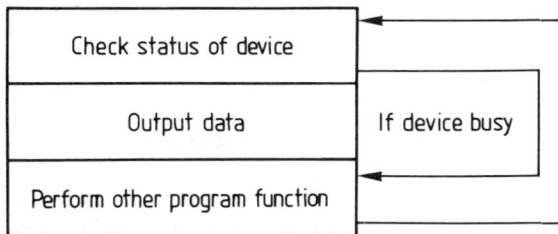

(b) Software

Figure 2.1 Software polling of output peripheral device

processing one data item. There are two mechanisms for handling this timing inconsistency and initiating data transfers between CPU and input/output.

(a) Software polling
In this technique a program initiates all data transfers between CPU and peripheral devices. Figure 2.1 demonstrates the principle.

The program which 'drives' the peripheral device, e.g., transfers data items to be processed by the peripheral device, must first check if the device is ready to receive data. This is termed 'polling' the device and involves reading the single input signal Device Status. This signal may be high to indicate that the device is ready to receive data or low to indicate that the device is busy, perhaps processing the previous data item. This polling may be (1) continuous or (2) periodic if the CPU performs another program function between regular checks on the status of the device, as shown in Fig. 2.1(b).

While Fig. 2.1 shows an output peripheral device only, e.g., a printer, VDU, or plotter, the same configuration applies for an input device, e.g., a keyboard, with the direction of data transfer reversed.

Typical labels which are given to the Device Status signal are:

BUSY for an output device like a printer and
DATA READY for an input device like a keyboard

(b) Interrupt driven
In this technique it is not the program which initiates data transfer. Instead the peripheral device generates a signal when it is ready for data transfer; this signal 'interrupts' the program which the CPU is running. Figure 2.2 demonstrates the principle.

The interrupt signal from the peripheral device is connected to one of several interrupt lines which comprise part of the control bus. When it is set it

9

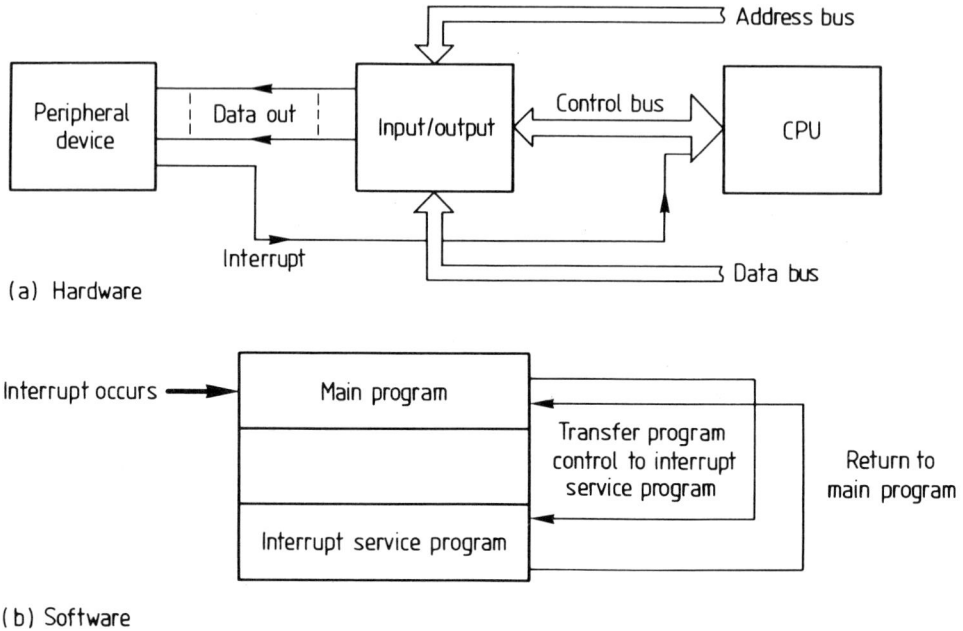

(a) Hardware

(b) Software

Figure 2.2 Interrupt driven output peripheral device

causes program control to be transferred from the program which is currently being executed and the interrupt service program is entered. This program then services the peripheral, e.g., inputs data from the peripheral, and when it is completed control is transferred back to the main program. Thus an instantaneous response is made by the program to the externally generated interrupt.

A mechanism must exist for storing the contents of the work registers (Accumulator, B, C, etc.) and the program counter contents when the main program is interrupted. If this is not done the interrupt service program will use and therefore overwrite the work registers. Also, when the interrupt program is completed the return point in the main program will be lost. Different methods for performing these functions and for generating the start address in memory of the interrupt service program will be described in a later chapter on interrupts (Chapter 4).

Examples

1. Sketch the hardware configuration for a microcomputer drive to a printer which incorporates two control signals — Request to Send from the microcomputer and Busy from the printer. Also, write a program to output an eight-bit character to the peripheral; use the Intel 8085 mnemonics given in the Appendix.

Answer: (a) Hardware: (*see figure top of opposite page*)

(b) Software. (Assume that the eight-bit character is output from a port with the input/output address hex. 10. Request to Send has an address of hex. 20 and the input signal Busy is connected to address hex. 30.)

```
      MVI   A,01H ⎫ Set Request to Send
      OUT   20H   ⎭
POLL : IN    30H     Wait loop until
      JNZ   POLL   Busy is set low
      MVI   A,36H ⎫ Output character
      OUT   10H   ⎭
```

Notice that the Busy signal is set (or not set) by the peripheral device upon receipt of a Request to Send signal which the program generates. This is termed 'handshaking'. The request to send signal could:

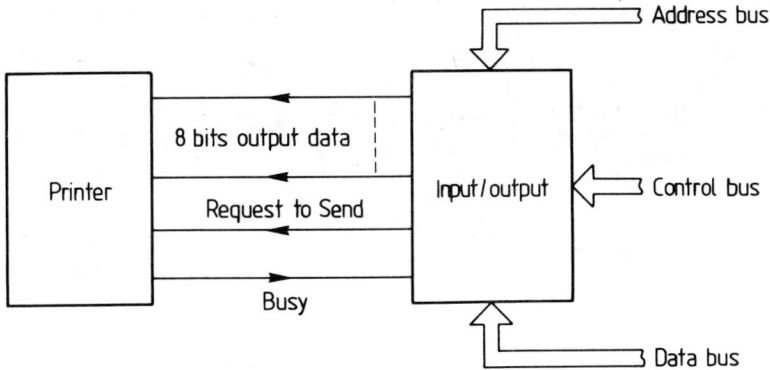

(1) Switch on the peripheral device or prime it to prepare to receive data;

(2) Ask the peripheral if it has data to send if it is an input device, e.g., a keyboard; the signal may then be termed 'Data to Send?'.

2. Show how two keyboards, which are under interrupt control, can be connected to a microcomputer.

Answer: (*see figure foot of page*)

3. Show how an A/D (analogue to digital) converter can be connected to a microcomputer, and write a program to poll the device and read the digital signal.

Answer: (a) Hardware: (*see figure top of next page*)

The A/D chip converts the analogue signal into an eight-bit digital value (10- or 12-bit converters are available for greater resolution). Conversion time may be 10 μs for the fastest type of converter or 1 ms for a cheaper and slower device.

Each conversion process is triggered by the Start Conversion signal, the Conversion Complete signal being generated when the process is terminated.

(b) Software. (Assume input/output addresses of hex. 00, 01, and 02 for the digital value, Start Conversion, and Conversion Complete respectively.)

```
        MVI  A,01H  }Set start
        OUT  01H    }conversion
POLL :  IN   02H    ⎫Wait loop until
        JZ   POLL   ⎬Conversion complete
                    ⎭is set
        IN   00H    Place eight-bit digital
                    value in accumulator
```

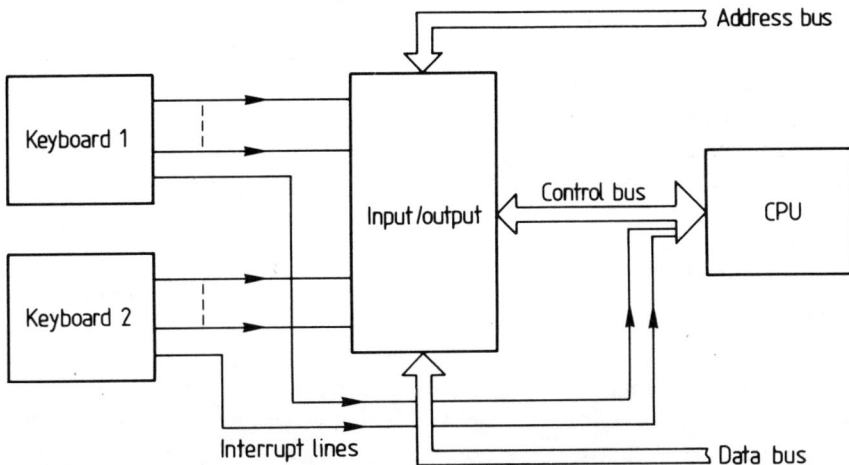

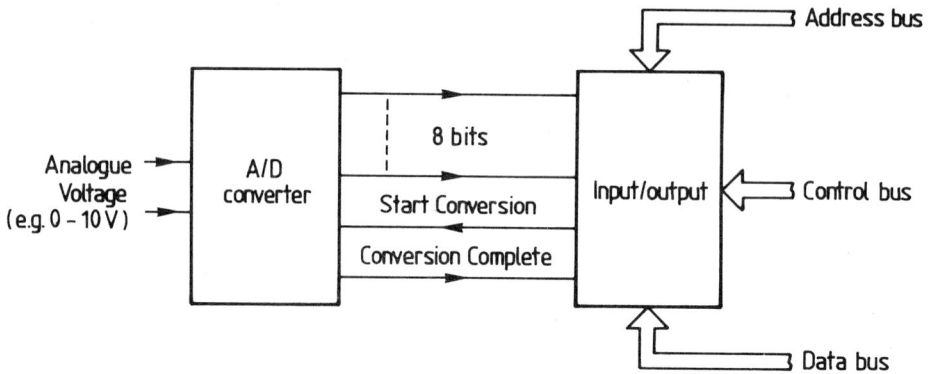

4. Show how an additional IC (or circuit) can be used to stop CPU operation and transfer data between memory and input/output directly (this is called DMA — direct memory access).

Answer:

controller the data source and destination addresses in memory and on disk, and the DMA controller implements the transfer when the disk has rotated to the required position.

5. Show how an input/output chip can be 'initialized' so that each port can be set to operate in the input or output mode.

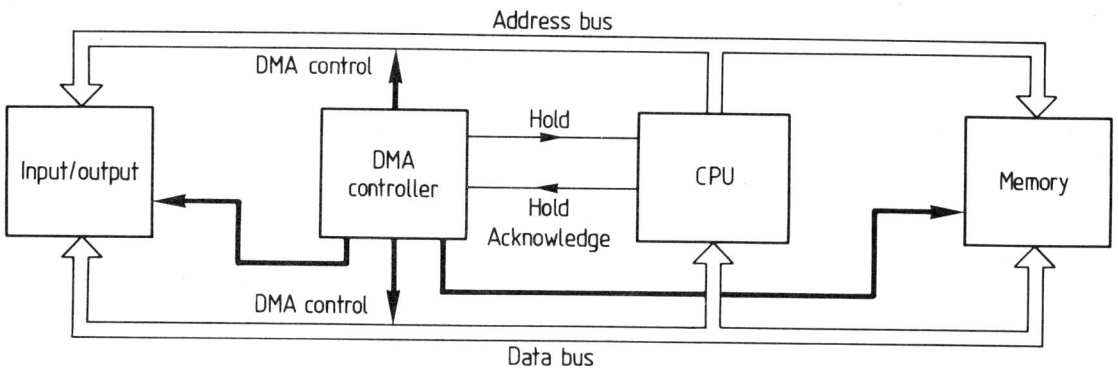

The DMA controller presents a Hold signal to the CPU, which responds with the Hold Acknowledge signal. The DMA controller then assumes control of the address and data busses and transfers data between memory and input/output *without* that data passing through the CPU. When a block of data has been transferred from memory to input/output, for instance, the CPU is released to continue program operation by the resetting of the Hold signal.

DMA allows very fast data transfers to be made, and is often used for communication to floppy disks. Typically a drive program gives the DMA

Answer:

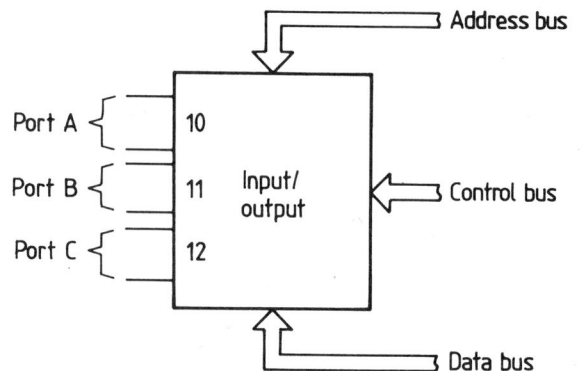

An additional address is available within this triple-port input/output IC to enable the device to be set for any particular input and output configuration:

Port A— Address 10 ⎫ |Determined by the
Port B— Address 11 ⎪ |settings on the
Port C— Address 12 ⎬ |two address lines
Control ⎪ |which are connected
register— Address 13 ⎭ |

A bit pattern is sent initially to the control register before input/output transfers are attempted, in order to define each port as either input or output, e.g.,

MVI A,82H
OUT 13H

might set ports A and C to operate in the output mode and port B to operate in the input mode. The precise bit pattern (hex. 82 in this case) must be determined from the manufacturer's data sheets for the device. Notice that this example is for the Intel 8255A.

Exercises

1. Place the following in order of speed of operation (fastest first):
   (a) printer (print 1 character) — 200 characters/second;
   (b) A/D converter (conversion time);
   (c) floppy disk access;
   (d) memory write.

2. If a VDU can process one data item (character) every 200 μs, how many program instructions can be implemented between successive data output operations — 1000, 40, 10, or 4000?

3. Which category of input/output is totally controlled by program?

4. What is wrong with the following section of program?
   MVI A,54H   Character 'T'
   OUT 10H   Output character to printer
   MVI A,45H   Character 'E'
   OUT 10H   Output character to printer

5. What is the 'status' of a peripheral device?

6. What action does an interrupt signal from a peripheral device perform?

7. What is 'initializing' a programmable input/output device?

8. Which of the following statements is true?
   (a) An interrupt signal causes the main program to be completed before program control is transferred to an interrupt routine.
   (b) The main program includes a jump instruction in order to enter an interrupt routine.
   (c) An interrupt causes an immediate response.

9. Write a program which continuously polls the peripheral device indicated in Fig. 2.1 and outputs eight zeros when the device is not busy. Assume that the eight-bit port has an input/output address of hex. 20 and that the single Device Status signal (set to 1 when busy) has an address of hex. 21.

10. What is 'handshaking'?

11. In addition to reading the state of an alarm contact (which requires immediate attention) in a plant, a microcomputer is required to perform a scan of several A/D converters, which involves considerable processing time. Which of the two methods of input/output control would you choose for the alarm contact and why?

12. Interrupt lines form part of which bus system?

13. What function must be performed when control is transferred from a main system program to an interrupt service program?

14. Sketch the hardware configuration for a VDU and keyboard parallel connection to a microcomputer, if:
    (a) The VDU output signal is eight-bit data plus one VDU Ready control signal.

(b) The keyboard signal is also eight bits with one interrupt signal Keyboard Ready.

15. Which software technique would you employ in a program which should continually output a stream of characters to a printer if no signal indicating printer status (busy or ready) is available? This technique should handle the speed incompatibility between microcomputer and printer.

16. What happens to a microprocessor when the control bus signal Hold is active?

17. State: (a) an advantage and (b) a disadvantage of using DMA for controlling data communication between a microcomputer and a floppy disk.

2.2 Interfacing circuitry

In the first part of this chapter and in the first book in this series covering Microelectronic Systems Levels I and II, several input/output configurations have been described. We have seen how input/output ports (eight-bit parallel input/output channels) are used to connect a microcomputer to the following devices:

(a) printer
(b) keyboard   } in Sec. 2.1
(c) A/D converter

(d) seven-segment display   } Microelectronic
(e) keyboard (detailed)   } Systems
(f) miscellaneous (loud-   } Levels I and II
speaker, lamp, switch)

In all cases the principal interfacing device is a single input/output IC.

A generalized representation of how such an interfacing device is used to drive peripheral equipment is shown in Fig. 2.3.

Port A consists of parallel latched (i.e., once set by program from the CPU to 0 or 1 the signal is staticized) output lines, which can be used to drive a whole range of output devices, e.g., printer, VDU, floppy disk, indicating lamps.

Port B carries eight parallel input signals which can be read by program into the CPU at any time;

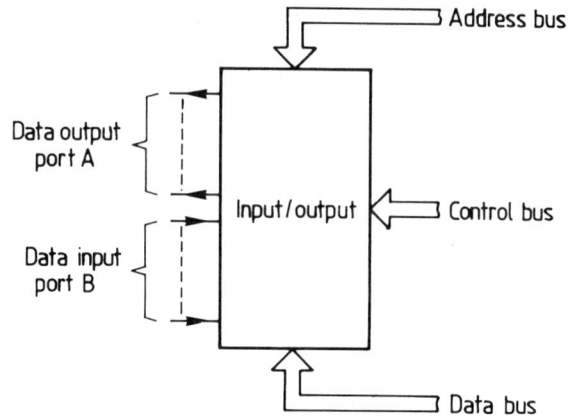

Figure 2.3 Generalized input/output configuration

these signals may feed from a keyboard, switch settings, floppy disk, etc.

Additional features which are often available are:
(a) A control register (with a different address to the port addresses) may exist on the input/output IC to enable the ports to be selected as input or output. This is uncommon with single-port devices but is common with two- or three-port devices.
(b) The third of the three ports on a device may be selected as a handshaking port. For instance, port C with the Intel 8255A can be set (by means of the control register) to use individual input and output lines, e.g., to output a Request to Transfer to a peripheral device and input a Device Busy signal from the device.

An IC which is often connected beyond the input/output IC is a 'decoder' chip, which is used to expand the number of output signal lines. Figure 2.4 demonstrates the mechanism and Table 2.1 gives a truth table for the device.

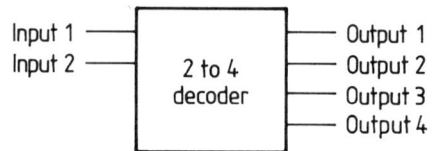

Figure 2.4 A 2 to 4 decoder chip

Only one of the output lines is set for any combination of input line settings. Therefore, a binary code on the input lines is expanded to set a

Table 2.1 Truth table for 2 to 4 decoder chip

Input 2	Input 1	Output 4	Output 3	Output 2	Output 1
0	0	0	0	0	1
0	1	0	0	1	0
1	0	0	1	0	0
1	1	1	0	0	0

discrete output line for each code. Thus a 3 to 8 decoder chip can be used to generate eight input/output signal lines from only three data bits into the device from an input/output IC. Example 8 will show the use of the device.

A further component which fits into the microcomputer configuration in the position of the input/output IC and which performs parallel to serial conversion (and vice versa) is a UART (universal asynchronous receiver transmitter — asynchronous because there is no synchronizing clock). This device is used to connect to remote devices using serial connection, i.e., data items are pulsed as a series of zeros and ones along a single wire (plus a 0 V reference) in each direction. Figure 2.5 shows the method of connection.

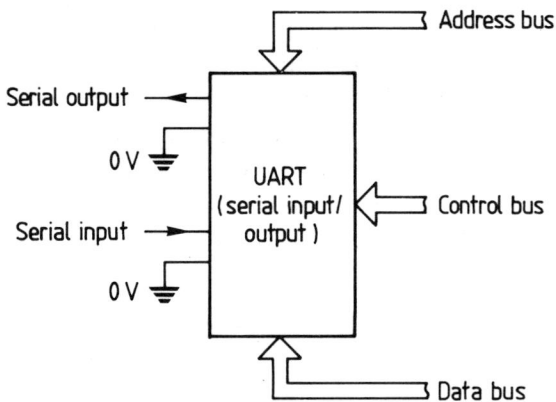

Figure 2.5 UART—serial input/output IC

Serial output is commonly applied to drive VDUs and printers, and serial input is often used with keyboards. The advantage is that only two wires in each direction are required for interconnection in place of eight (or nine to include a 0 V reference) for parallel connection. However, data transfer is slower for serial transmission; data are presented instantaneously on all signal lines for parallel transmission, but data bits are presented sequentially, with a time delay between bits, on a single line for serial transmission.

At the heart of the UART chip is a pair of 'shift registers' — one for each direction of data transfer. Each of these circuits operates in one of the following modes:
(a) Output: loaded in parallel by eight bits from the data bus. Each bit is shifted out at a fixed frequency to the remote peripheral.
(b) Input: loaded by serial pulses from the peripheral device. The assembled eight bits can then be read in parallel along the data bus into the CPU.

Examples

6. Sketch the hardware configuration for a four-port parallel drive to a VDU and keyboard. Handshaking is applied with both devices.
Answer: (see (1) on next page)

Clearly four ports plus bus connections cannot be supported on a single IC (40 pin maximum). Two or more ICs are required.

Parallel connection to a VDU is not as common as serial connection, which is described in the next example

7. (a) Show how a VDU and keyboard can be driven in serial form from a microcomputer.
   (b) Sketch the waveform of the serial signal.
   (c) Explain why a UART needs to be 'initialized'.
Answer: (a) *(see (2) on next page)*

In this arrangement the VDU and its associated keyboard, which comprise a single unit, possess a shared bidirectional UART within the device itself. This UART interposes the serial transmission signals T_x (transmit) and R_x (receive) and the parallel internal operation of the VDU/keyboard unit.

16

(1) *Answer to Example 6*

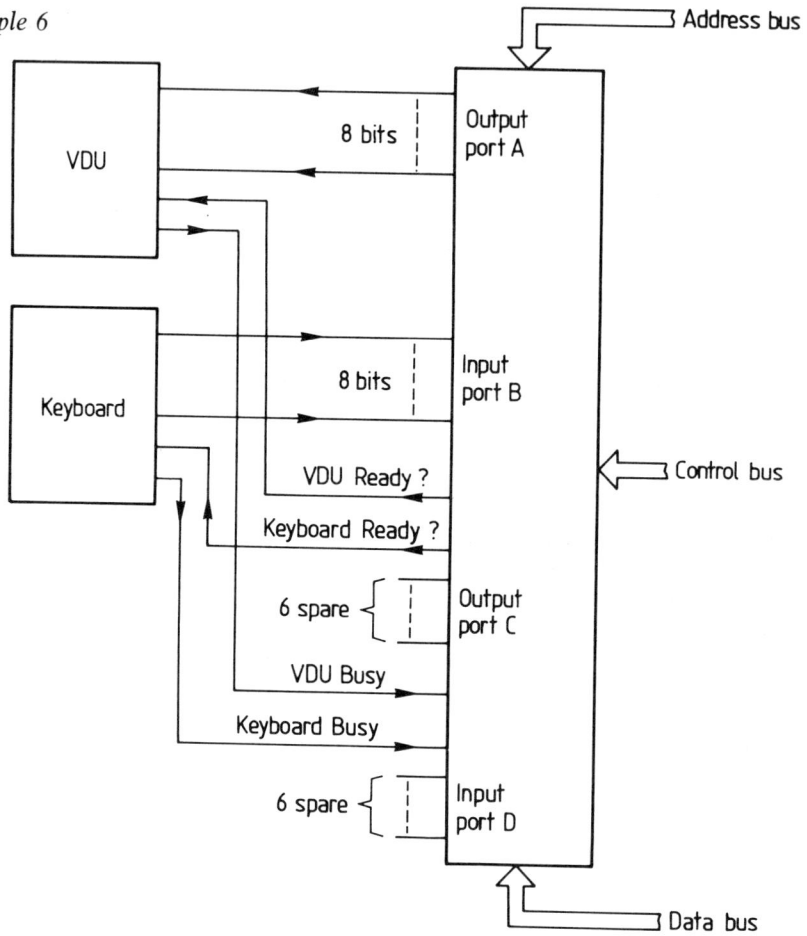

(2) *Answer to Example 7(a)*

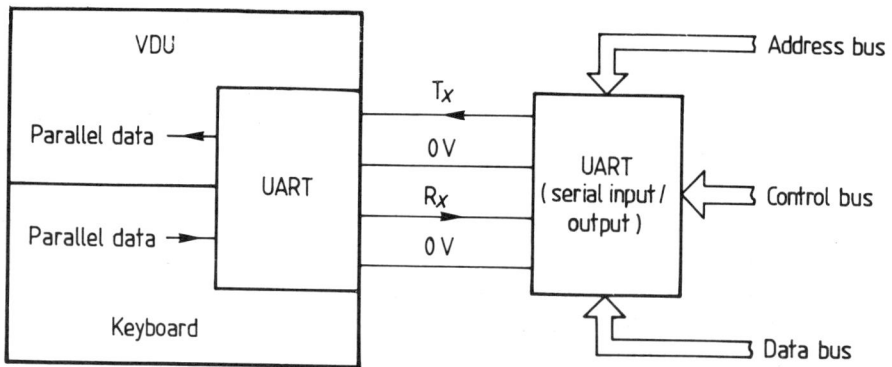

Logic 0

Logic 1

Start bit — 7 data bits — Parity bit — Stop bit

Answer to Example 7(b)

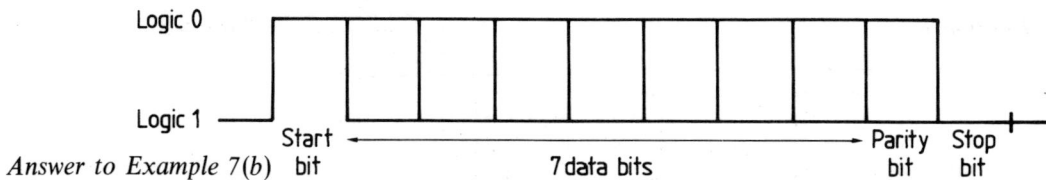

Invariably data are transferred serially between microcomputers and peripheral devices using the ASCII code. This is an eight-bit code for each of the alphabet letters, numbers, etc., comprising seven data bits plus one parity bit. If even parity is selected, the parity bit is set to 1 if the number of ones in the first seven bits is odd. The waveform is framed by start and stop bits (sometimes two stop bits are selected).

The transmission speed is measured in *baud* (bits per second) and must be set precisely at the transmit and receive ends. Standard baud rates are 110, 300, 600, 1200, 2400, 4800, and 9600. Faster rates for intercomputer links are available. A slow printer may operate at 300 baud (i.e., 30 characters per second) and a VDU at 2400 baud.

An international standard specification for serial links exists. This is termed the RS 232-C interface and describes:

(1) signal levels (e.g., logic $1 =$ approx. -9 V

logic $0 =$ approx. $+9$ V);

(2) bit patterns (as above);
(3) baud rates (as above);
(4) pin connections and control/handshaking signals (e.g., on a 25-pin connector T_x is pin 2, R_x is pin 3, 0 V is pin 7, Request to Send is pin 4, etc.)

(c) 'Initializing' a UART is the process of setting the device to the required RS 232-C options before data are transferred, e.g.:

(1) baud rate (T_x and R_x);
(2) parity (odd or even);
(3) number of stop bits (one or two);
(4) number of data bits (invariably seven)

This procedure is accomplished by software by sending control data bytes to the UART from the CPU before the UART is used in its transmit and receive modes. Therefore a UART effectively contains a control register, as used by some parallel input/output ICs.

8. Show how two 3 to 8 decoder ICs allow only six output lines to be expanded to generate 16 discrete signals.

Answer: (see (1) on next page)

Thus if an output code of 6 zeros is sent by program to the port, the top output signal line is set.

The 16 output signals can be used to light lamps, energize relays, drive peripheral devices, etc. However, there is a limitation that only one of each set of eight outputs can be set at any time.

9. (a) Show how a group of four manual switches and four indicator lamps can be connected to a microcomputer.

   (b) Draw a flow chart and write a program to light the indicator lamps in response to the settings of the switches.

Answer: (a) (see (2) on next page)

Logic 0 (or 0 V) is presented on each input pin when the manual switches S1 to S4 are in their normally open state; these voltage levels are obtained through the resistors R1 to R4. When any switch is closed, logic 1 ($+5$ V) is presented on its input pin.

To light any of the indicator lamps L1 to L4, a logic 0 must be set on its output pin — the drivers provide bit inversion. Thus $+5$ V is set across the lamp in order to illuminate it.

The primary function of the drivers (typically, eight are mounted on a single IC) is to provide sufficient current drive for the lamps and to prevent an electrical overload on the input/output IC. If too much current is demanded by a loading circuit on one of the output pins on this IC, the device may be damaged.

(b) Flow chart: *(see (3) at top of page 19)*

18

(1) *Answer to Example 8*

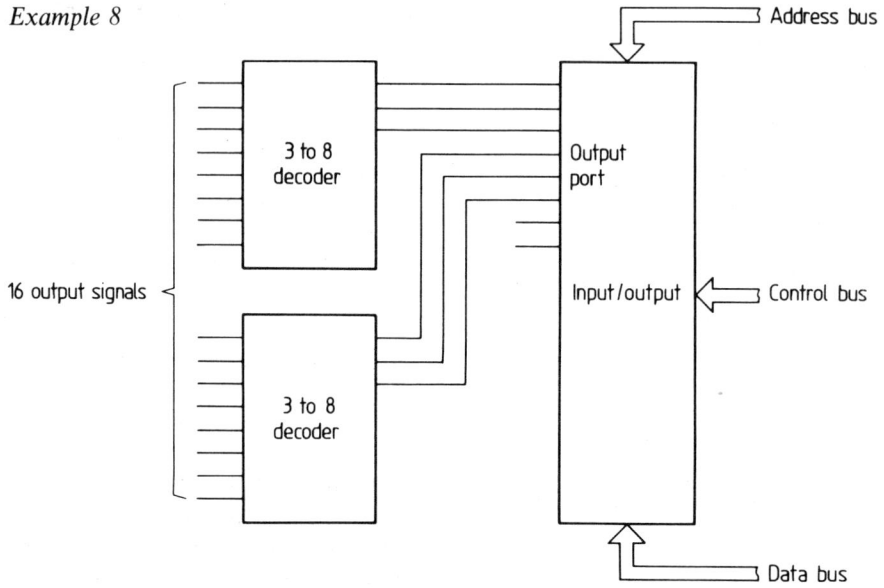

(2) *Answer to Example 9(a)*

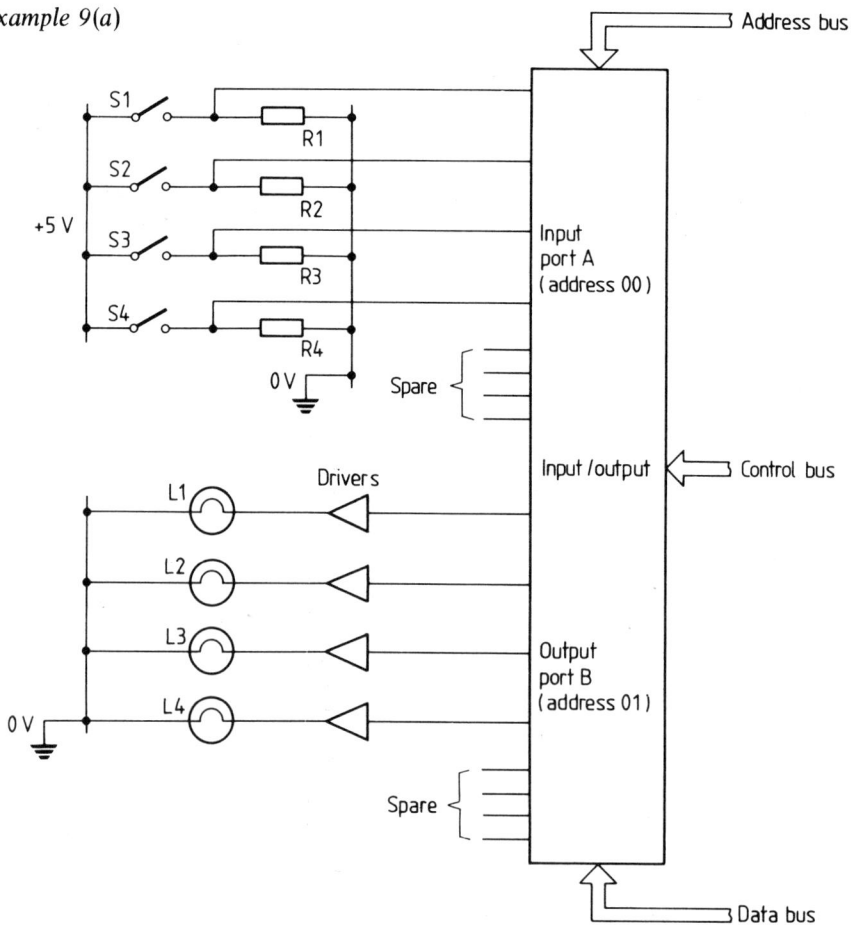

(3) *Answer to Example 9(b)*

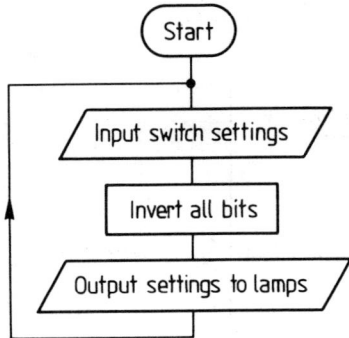

Program:

```
START: IN  00H    Input switch settings
                  to accumulator
       CMA        Complement (invert all
                  bits) accumulator
       OUT 01H    Output switch settings
                  to lamps
       JMP START  Repeat program
```

The program continuously scans the keyboard and drives the indicator lamps. If any switch is closed the corresponding lamp lights.

10. Show how a special function input/output IC can interface to a floppy disk.

Answer:

The disk surface is divided into several (typically 77) concentric tracks; each track consists of several sectors (typically 256). There are several bytes in each sector.

The Write Data and Read Data signals show that data are written to and read from disk in serial form. The controller IC frames these bit streams into parallel bytes for transfer to and from the microcomputer bus systems (usually under DMA control, of course).

The controller uses the index pulse, which is generated as the disk rotates, to determine the sector position of the read/write head. The head moves only in a radial direction, and Track 0 is a reference signal.

When the drive software requires to make a disk transfer, a disk address (track and sector numbers) is sent to the controller. The controller uses the Head Step and Head Direction signals to position the read/write head on the required track. The controller knows when the disk has rotated to present the required sector under the read/write head by its monitoring of the index pulse. The Head Load signal is then generated, which places the head in contact with the rotating disk surface. Simultaneously data transfers are initiated, e.g., the DMA Request, or Hold, signal is set on the CPU's control bus.

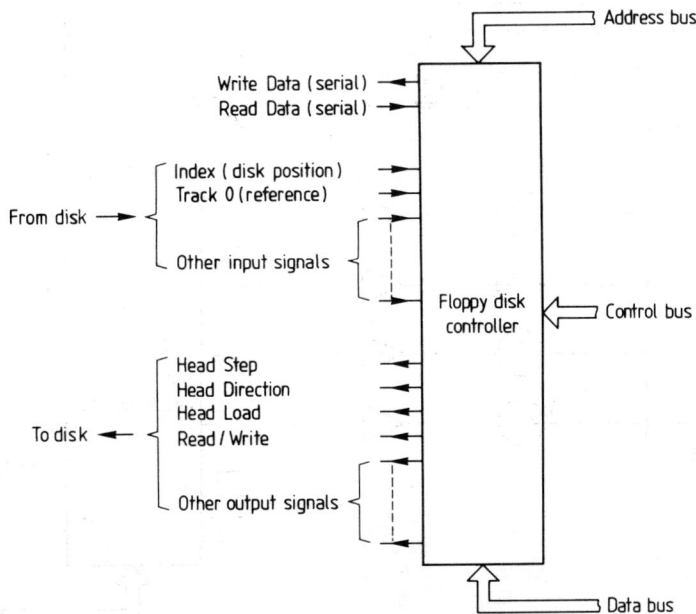

11. Show how a simple 74LS373 tri-state 'octal latch' IC can be used as an output or input port.

Answer: (a) Output:

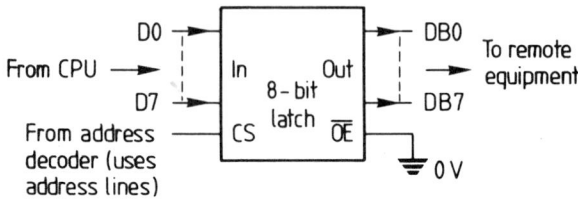

The device is connected to the data bus and a chip select is generated from an address decoding circuit. If the Output Enable signal ($\overline{\text{OE}}$) is not set to 0, the output signals DB0 to DB7 are in the 'floating' state, i.e., cannot be set to 0 or 1. Therefore, $\overline{\text{OE}}$ is set permanently to 0 so that data bus signals are transmitted through the device (as well as latched, or staticized) when the chip select is active.

(b) Input:

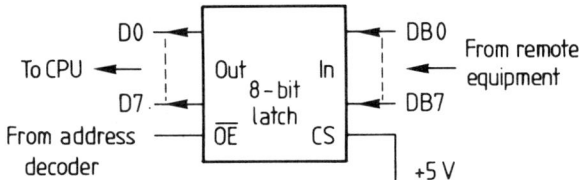

In this case the external signal lines DB0 to DB7 are connected to the input pins. The chip select pin is set to +5 V (permanent enable), but the Output Enable signal is used to perform the chip select function, as selected by an address decoder circuit. Thus data are only presented onto the data bus when the device is selected by an input instruction which includes the appropriate input/output address.

12. Demonstrate the action of a special function keyboard control chip, which scans automatically the key settings and generates a code when any key is pressed.

Answer: (*see figure top of next column*)

When a key is pressed the IC generates an eight-bit code which can be read by software along the data bus into the CPU. Often an interrupt signal is available, and this can be used to trigger an interrupt program, which reads the data code when

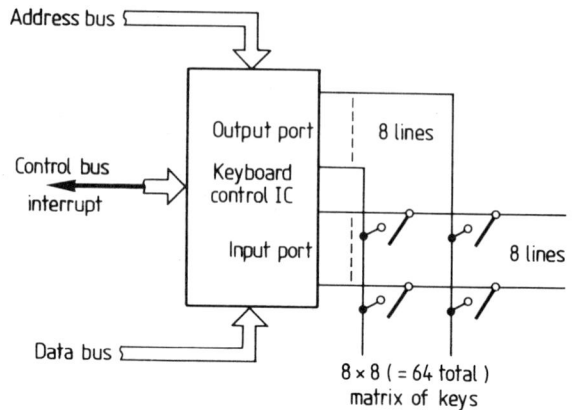

a key is pressed.

Thus the keyboard is 'scanned' by hardware. This avoids the necessity of providing a program routine which sets each of the output lines in turn and reads in the settings of the matrixed input signals in order to determine which (if any) key is pressed.

Exercises

18. What is an input/output port?

19. What are peripheral 'status' signals?

20. What is a 'latched' output bit?

21. What is the function of a 'control register' on a programmable input/output IC?

22. Which is faster: serial or parallel data transfer?

23. Why is it not possible to package a double-port input/output IC in a 24-pin DIL?

24. Sketch a diagram which shows how the following devices can be connected to a microcomputer:
    (a) LED (light emitting diode) — output:

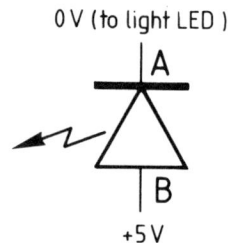

Connect a driver, which provides bit inversion, to A and connect B to +5 V.

(b) Electrical relay — output:

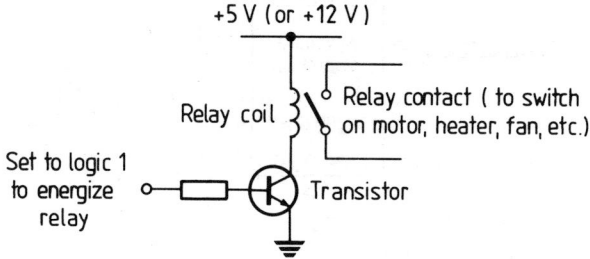

The transistor circuit is a discrete component replacement for an IC driver. By correct choice of components it can energize a heavy-duty relay.

(c) Loudspeaker — output:

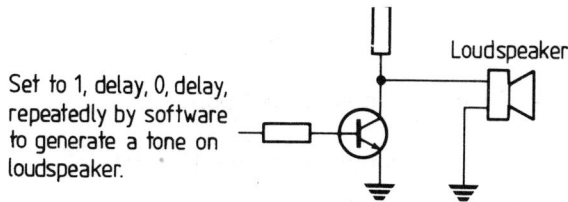

(d) Pushbutton — input:

25. Draw the truth table for a 3 to 8 decoder.

26. What code must be output to the input/output port in Example 8 to set only the first and the last of the 16 output signals?

27. What do the initials UART stand for?

28. What is a shift register?

29. How many characters can be sent by serial link per second to a VDU at a baud rate of 4800; one stop bit is used.

30. Draw a diagram which shows how two microcomputers can be connected together by serial link.

31. Would you use serial or parallel connection to the following peripherals (give reasons):
    (a) a printer which is sited 500 metres from the microcomputer;
    (b) a VDU, which is sited adjacent to the microcomputer, and which must receive a screen update (2000 characters) in less than 1 second.

32. Write a program which will illuminate light L2 in Example 9 when switch S1 is open.

33. Identify three errors in the following RS 232-C timing waveform:

    (*see figure foot of page*)

34. Identify the two control bus signals which are connected to a floppy disk controller chip when DMA is applied (you may need to refer to Sec. 2.1).

35. It is required to connect two outputs ports to a microcomputer in order to drive 16 remote relays. What is a cheaper alternative solution to using a three-port programmable input/output IC?

36. What is the advantage of connecting a keyboard to a 'keyboard encoder' IC rather than to a programmable input/output IC?

37. Why does a 40-pin VLSI IC, which performs a floppy disk controller function, possess a serial/parallel converter?

38. What is the function of the Head Load signal in a floppy disk controller?

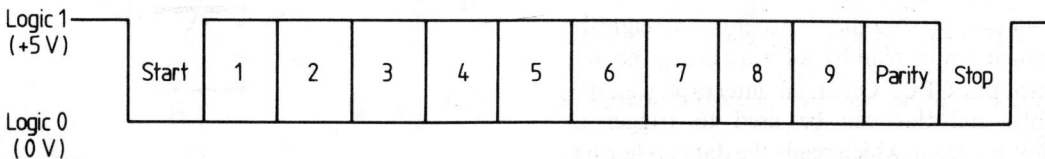

3 Subroutines and stack

3.1 Subroutines

Often a series of program instructions is required more than once in a program. In this case it is sensible to segregate that section of program into a 'subroutine'. The subroutine is placed in memory outside the program and can be called more than once from the main program. Figure 3.1 demonstrates the principle.

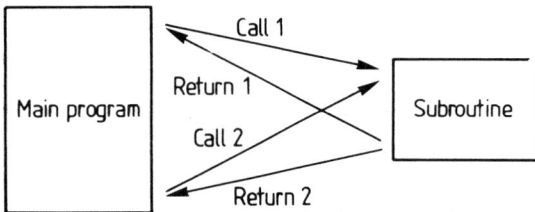

Figure 3.1 Subroutine calling

The subroutine is entered with a CALL instruction, and the last instruction within the subroutine is always a RETURN instruction. RETURN transfers program control back to the instruction which follows the CALL instruction in the main program.

Structuring a program into a main section plus one or more subroutines facilitates program testing. It is easier to understand and debug a program which is modular in this way.

Subroutines can be used for functions such as input/output transfers, time delay, particular mathematical operations, etc. Often it is necessary to pass data from the calling program for use within the subroutine. This can be performed within one of the work registers (e.g., the accumulator) or in a chosen memory location.

The CPU must possess a facility to store the return address when a main program calls a subroutine. This mechanism is described in Sec. 3.2.

22

Examples

1. Demonstrate the machine code instructions CALL and RETURN using the Intel 8085 instruction set (see Appendix).

Answer: In principle:

Memory Address

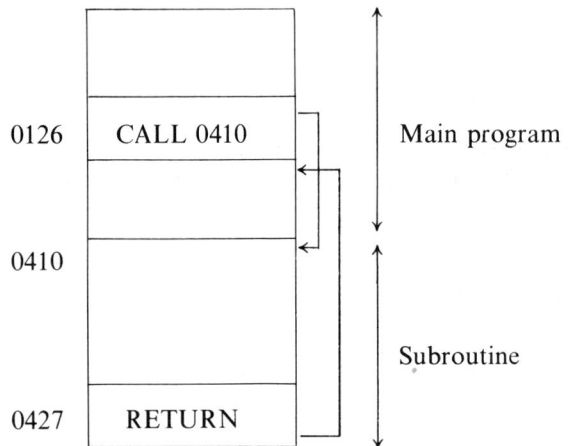

In detail:

Memory Address

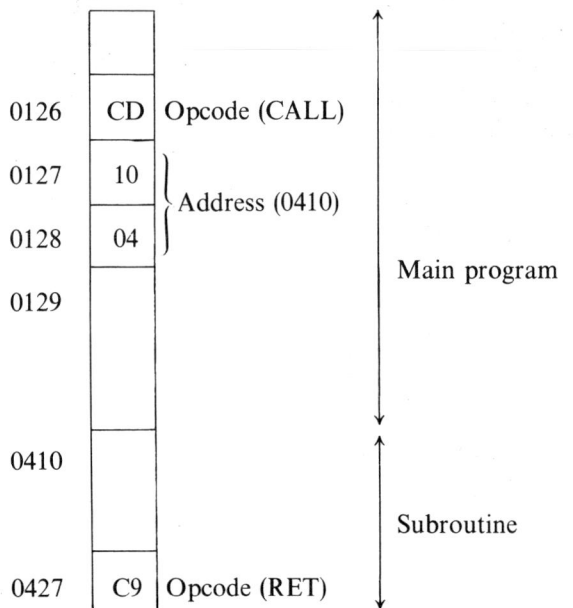

The RET instruction transfers program control back to memory address 0129.

2. Show how a time delay subroutine can be utilized within a program.

Answer:

Label	Operator	Operand	Comments
	CALL	DELAY	Enter subroutine DELAY
DELAY:	MVI	A,100	Load A with 100
LOOP:	DCR	A	
	JNZ	LOOP	Loop 100 times
	RET		Return to main program

The time delay can be variable if a delay count is passed from the main program to the subroutine, as follows:

Label	Operator	Operand	Comments
	MVI	A,100	Load A with delay count
	CALL	DELAY	Enter subroutine DELAY
DELAY:	DCR A		Loop the number of times
	JNZ	DELAY	held in A
	RET		Return to main program

This second subroutine is therefore more general than the first. This mechanism of setting data into registers or memory locations within the main program for use in the subroutine is sometimes called 'parameter passing'.

3. Write a subroutine which flashes a light (port address 02) when it is called.

Answer:

Label	Operator	Operand	Comments
FLASH:	MVI	A,01	Set right-hand bit in A to 1
	OUT	02H	Output to port address 02
	MVI	A,10	
DELAY:	DCR	A	Time delay
	JNZ	DELAY	
	MVI	A,00	Set right-hand bit in A to 0
	OUT	02H	Output to port address 02
	RET		Return to main program

Every time the subroutine FLASH is called, the light is illuminated, a short delay occurs, and then the light is extinguished.

4. Write a subroutine which multiplies the two numbers 10 and 5 which are held in memory locations 0100 and 0101 respectively.

Answer:

Label	Opcode	Operand	Comments
MULT:	LDA	0100H	Load A with 10 (held in location 100)
	MOV	B,A	Transfer to B
	LDA	0101H	Load A with 5 (held in location 101)
	MOV	C,A	Transfer to C
	MOV	A,0	Clear A
LOOP:	ADD	C	Add C to A
	DCR	B	Decrement loop count (10 initially)
	JNZ	LOOP	Repeat
	RET		Return to main program

The product must not be a large number to avoid overflowing the eight-bit accumulator.

Notice that this particular technique for multiplying two numbers consumes a relatively large amount of CPU time, e.g., the program loops 10 times. A better but more complicated technique involves shifting (e.g., one place left to multiply by 2, two places left to multiply by 4, etc.) and adding the partial products. For example, to multiply a number by 5, shift it left two places and add the original number.

Exercises

1. What instruction is used to call a subroutine?

2. Which of the following statements about the use of a calculation subroutine, called three times in a program, is true?
   (a) improves program readability;
   (b) lengthens object code;
   (c) improves program structure;
   (d) increases the program running time;
   (e) alters the contents of the work registers which are used in the main program.
   Explain your answer to (d).

3. Why is the return address important to a subroutine?

4. What is wrong with the following instruction which is placed at the end of a subroutine?

    RET   010EH   Return to address 010E

5. What is wrong with the following program?

```
TOM      : MVI   B,0
           CALL  DICK
CHARLIE  : JMP   HARRY
DICK     : INR   C
           INR   D
           JMP   TOM
           RET
HARRY    : LDA   0025H
              |
              |
              |
             etc.
```

6. Which of the following two program sections is sensibly segregated into a subroutine which is called twice from the main program?

   (a) MVI A,1
         OUT 03H

   (b) a program section which performs 16-bit addition and checks the answer against limits.

       Justify your selection.

7. Write a program which sets a data byte of hex. 40 in memory location 1000 and then calls a subroutine. The subroutine examines this memory location and outputs a 1 to light a LED at port address 01 if the data byte is hex. 40. It then returns to the main program.

8. Write a subroutine which examines a list of 10 data values, which are loaded in memory commencing at location 1000, and places the largest value in the C register.

3.2 Stack

Most microprocessors use a *stack* to store return addresses when subroutines are called. The stack is normally any reserved set of memory locations, although a limited stack is contained within the CPU in the case of one or two microprocessors. The CPU records the memory address of the stack within a 16-bit register called the *stack pointer*, which resides within the CPU.

The stack mechanism would be unnecessary if it could be guaranteed that only one subroutine call would be made in a program; this address could be stored in a single register within the CPU. However, if a subroutine calls another subroutine, a *nested* subroutine system would exist, as shown in Fig. 3.2.

In this arrangement two return addresses must be stored in subroutine 2. Higher order nesting is possible and therefore there is a requirement for an expandable storage area (in memory) to hold return addresses.

The mechanism of the stack and stack pointer system is demonstrated in Fig. 3.3.

When the CALL instruction is implemented in the main program, the subroutine is entered, and the return address is stored on the stack. The 16-bit CPU register, the stack pointer, holds the address of the last-used stack location in memory. When the RET instruction is implemented at the end of the subroutine, the return address is transferred off the stack into the CPU's program counter.

The stack pointer is automatically decremented and incremented as return addresses are placed on the stack and later removed from the stack during subroutine calls. The stack therefore operates on a 'last-in-first-out' basis.

The use of the stack in this way is fully automatic as far as the programmer is concerned. He simply uses the CALL and RET instructions when using

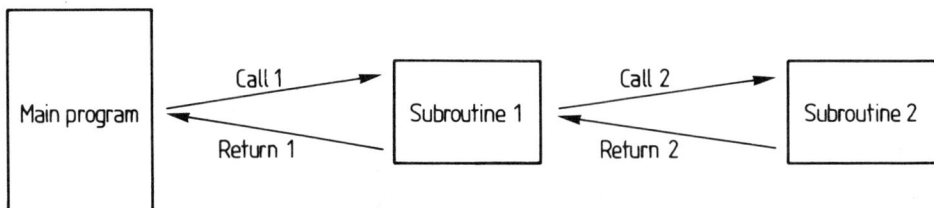

Figure 3.2 Nested subroutines

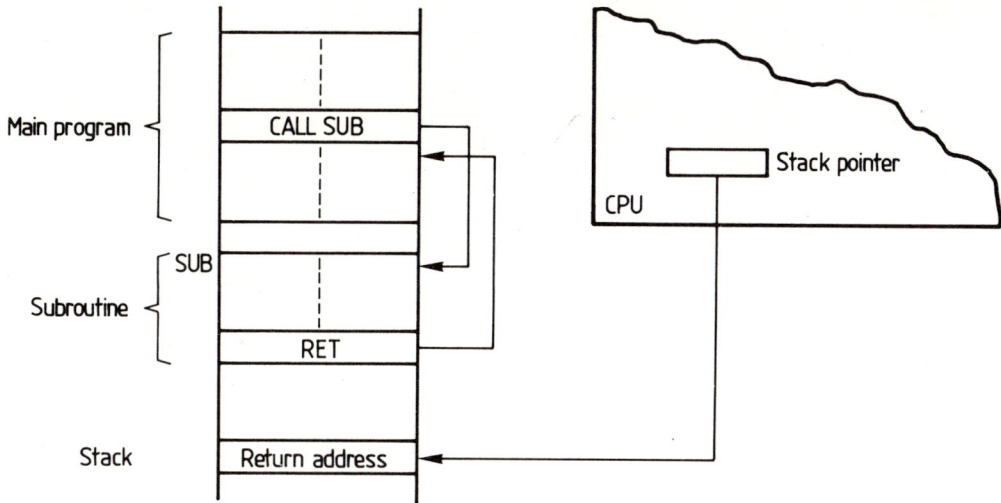

Figure 3.3 The stack and stack pointer

subroutines and allows the CPU and its stack pointer to handle the return addressing. However, he can use the stack manually, i.e., he can use it to place 16-bit data values or addresses onto the stack and later retrieve them from the stack. The instructions which he uses are:

PUSH—place a number or address onto the stack
POP—retrieve the number

e.g., PUSH B places the contents of the register-pair B and C onto the stack and POP B retrieves the 16-bit data value.

Examples

5. Show the state of a stack, which expands backwards through memory, at each stage in the following nested subroutine system.

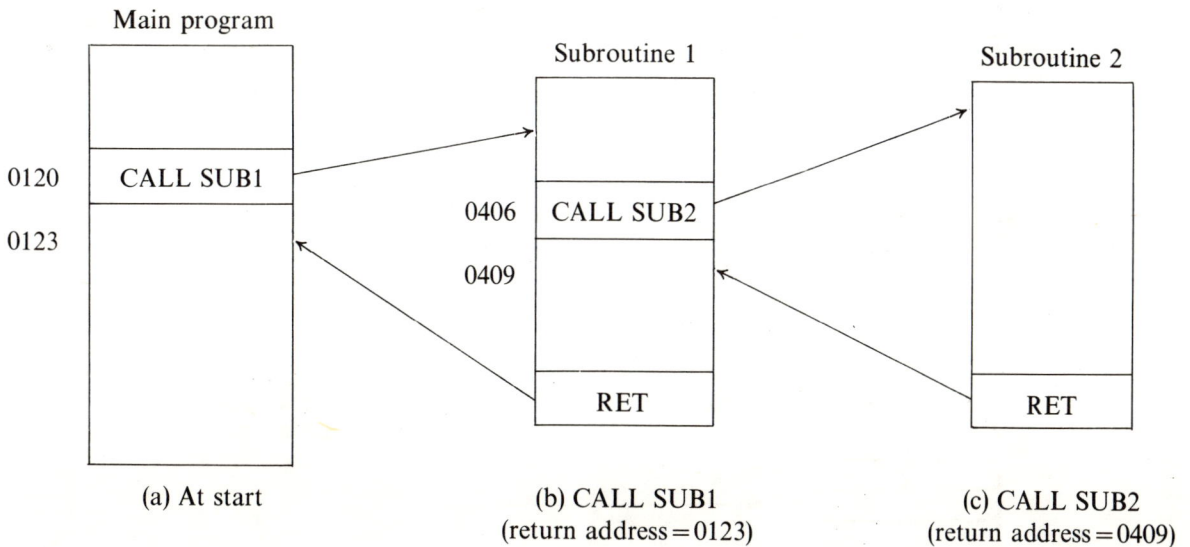

Main program	
0120	CALL SUB1
0123	

(a) At start

0406	CALL SUB2
0409	
	RET

(b) CALL SUB1
(return address = 0123)

Subroutine 2

RET

(c) CALL SUB2
(return address = 0409)

Assume that the stack pointer (SP) is set initially to 2008.

the registers and the main program wishes to prevent over-writing.

Answer:

(a)

2008	← SP

(b)

2006	23	← SP
2007	01	
2008		

(c)

2004	09	← SP
2005	04	
2006	23	
2007	01	
2008		

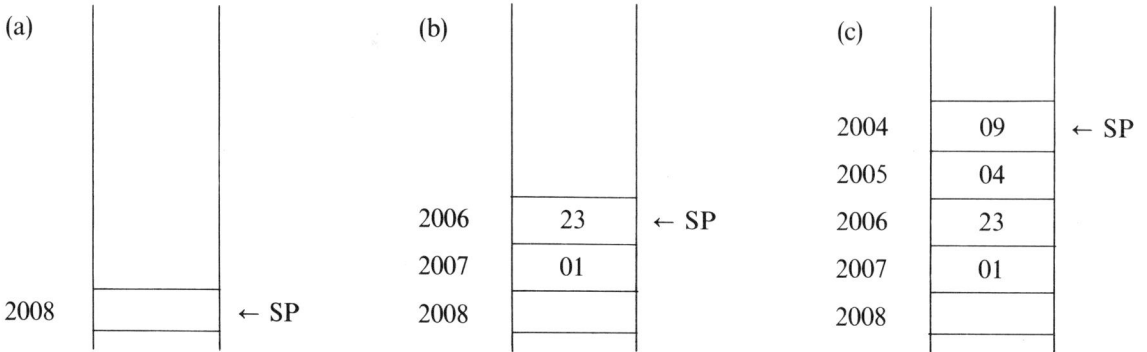

6. Show on a memory map the contents of all relevant memory locations when a subroutine call is made from address 2026. The subroutine start and end addresses are 304A and 3063, and the stack pointer is set initially at 400C. Use the Intel instruction set (see the Appendix).

Answer: see figure at foot of page

7. Write a program which saves the contents of all registers on the stack before a subroutine is called and retrieves them on return. This is sometimes necessary when the subroutine uses some or all of

Answer:

PUSH	PSW	Store A and status register on stack
PUSH	B	Store B and C
PUSH	D	Store D and E
PUSH	H	Store H and L
CALL	SUB	Call subroutine
POP	H	Retrieve H and L
POP	D	Retrieve D and E
POP	B	Retrieve B and C
POP	PSW	Retrieve A and status register

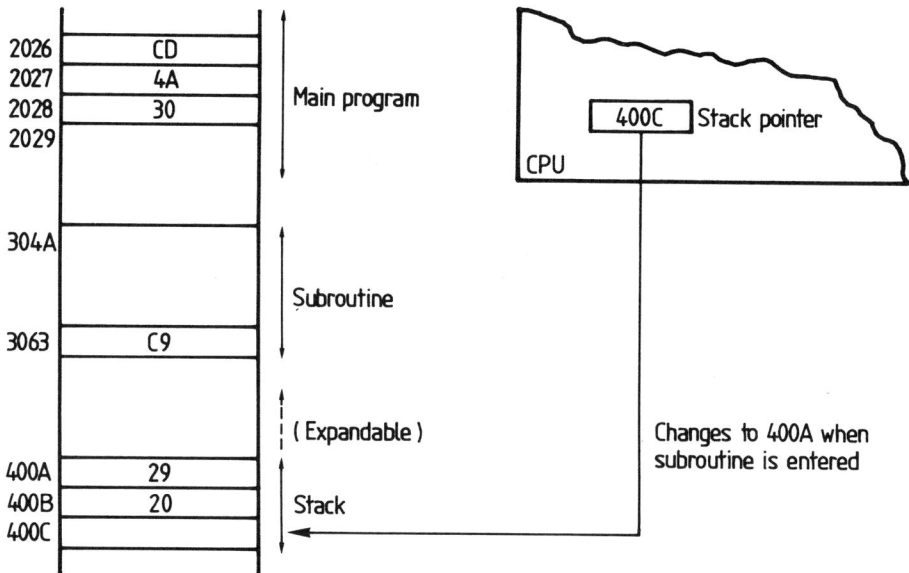

Address	Contents	
2026	CD	Main program
2027	4A	
2028	30	
2029		
304A		Subroutine
3063	C9	
		(Expandable)
400A	29	
400B	20	Stack
400C		

CPU — 400C Stack pointer

Changes to 400A when subroutine is entered

Notice that data are recalled off the stack in reverse order from that in which they are stored.

Exercises

9. What is a nested subroutine?

10. Why is it not necessary to use a PUSH instruction to place the return address on the stack when a subroutine is called?

11. Is there any limit to stack size?

12. Where is the stack normally located?

13. Which CPU register indicates the last stack location which is used, and what is its length?

14. The instruction which the Intel 8085 uses normally to set up the stack pointer (generally performed at the start of the main program) is:

LXI SP, STACK Load stack pointer with address STACK

What is wrong with the following?

LXI SP, 000H

15. What is wrong with the following program?

```
         |
         |
         CALL   SETDATA   Call subroutine
         |
         |
SETDATA: MVI     A,01H     Set 01 in A
         LXI     B,0102H   Set 02 in B and 03 in C
         PUSH    B         Store B and C on stack
         RET               Return to main program
```

16. Draw a memory map showing the state of the stack and the stack pointer at each of the stages (a) to (d) in the operation of the following program. The stack pointer is set initially at 0020.

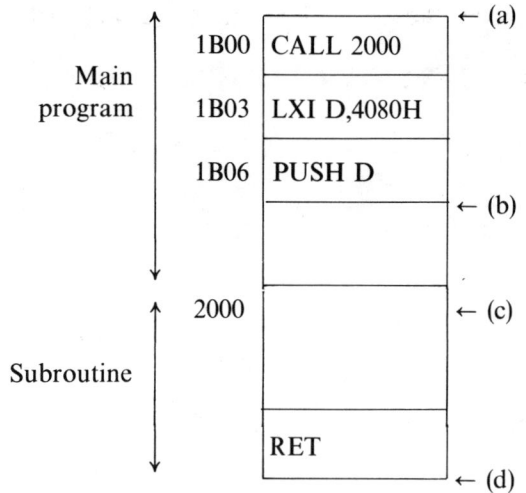

		← (a)
1B00	CALL 2000	
1B03	LXI D,4080H	
1B06	PUSH D	← (b)
2000		← (c)
	RET	← (d)

Main program / Subroutine

What is the final setting of the stack pointer and what are the contents of the top location in the stack?

17. The following program provides temporary storage of the contents of the B, C, D, and E registers in a data table commencing at location 4000:

```
LXI    H,4000H   Load HL register pair with address 4000
MOV    M,B       Move B to memory (4000)
INX    H         Increment HL
MOV    M,C       Move C to memory (4001)
INX    H         Increment HL
MOV    M,D       Move D to memory (4002)
INX    H         Increment HL
MOV    M,E       Move E to memory (4003)
```

Write an equivalent program which uses the stack for data storage. How many memory bytes are saved?

18. A main program calls subroutine A, which calls subroutine B, which calls itself once, i.e., it is 'recursive'. Can a stack handle this arrangement, and how many bytes in the stack are required?

19. State three ways in which data can be passed to a subroutine.

4 Interrupts

4.1 Interrupt action

Often the microcomputer must respond to external events which are unpredictable and require immediate attention. A peripheral device or a remote signal may demand that the microcomputer stops the program function which it is obeying currently and executes a separate interrupt program which services that device or signal.

Sometimes it is acceptable to software poll a manual keyboard, i.e., at regular intervals check if any key is pressed. However, if it is required to remove this software overhead and only scan the keyboard when a key is actually pressed, an interrupt signal must be generated for any key operation. A keyboard scan program is then entered. Figure 4.1 shows the mechanism of an interrupt.

The mechanism is almost identical to the use of a subroutine, e.g.:

(a) On entry, the program counter is overwritten with the start address of the interrupt program and the return address is placed on the stack.
(b) On completion, a RET instruction causes the return address to be transferred off the stack into the program counter.

The only difference is the method of entry. A subroutine is entered by the use of a software CALL instruction—software activated. An interrupt program is entered when an external hardware signal is set—hardware activated.

Notice that the interrupt program (often called an interrupt 'routine') can be entered at any point in the execution of the main program. It is virtually impossible to predict when a random external signal will occur and initiate the interrupt routine.

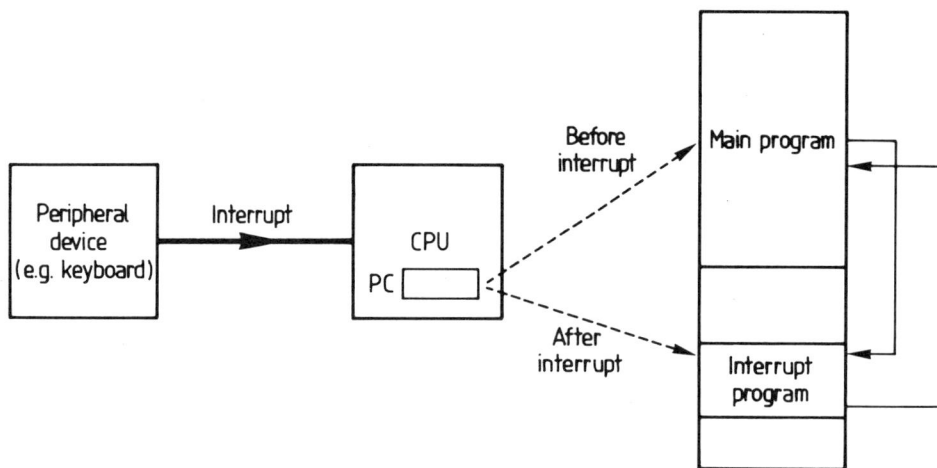

Figure 4.1 Interrupt mechanism

When the interrupt line is set, the main program completes the current instruction and then control is transferred to the interrupt program. When the interrupt program is complete, control is returned to the main program.

Typically, microprocessors have between four and eight interrupt lines, which can be considered to be part of the control bus. Nested interrupts can therefore occur. Commonly a priority system exists with multiple-interrupt systems, as shown in Fig. 4.2.

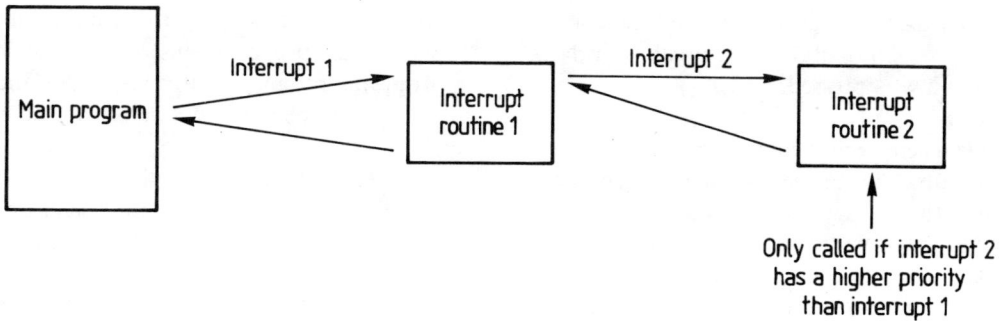

Figure 4.2 Nested interrupts

Some method must exist for storing the contents of the CPU's registers (e.g., A, B, C, D, E, H, and L) in addition to the program counter. This is more important with interrupt routines than with subroutines because it is not possible to estimate the precise point at which the main program will be interrupted. Registers can therefore be overwritten in a more unpredictable manner. The registers can be stored on the stack or elsewhere in memory; in some microprocessors a new set of registers can be selected.

Examples

1. List the commonly applied application of interrupt signals.
Answer: (a) Restart:

A manual key or pushbutton signal causes the main program to be restarted:

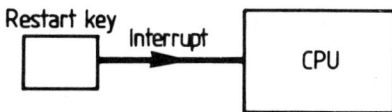

This is a useful facility in a training microcomputer or in a desktop computer which is based on a CRT or VDU, e.g., business system or program development system. The user's program may loop continuously or otherwise cause the master program to 'crash'. In this situation the method of restarting the main program is to interrupt the faulty program.

(b) Timer:

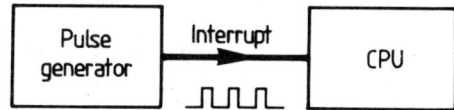

An internal timer circuit can interrupt the main program, e.g., at precise 10 ms intervals. This enables the interrupt routine to track 'real' time and to maintain a time-of-day clock in memory. Also, scanning of keyboards or plant signals can be initiated on a timed basis, e.g., every 100 ms or when the interrupt routine has counted 10 interrupt pulses.

(c) Floppy disk:

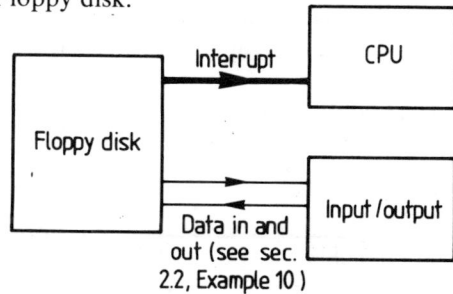

The microcomputer outputs a disk address (track and sector). The floppy disk controller interrupts the CPU when that address is located (typically 30 ms later) so that data transfers can be initiated.

(d) Keyboard:

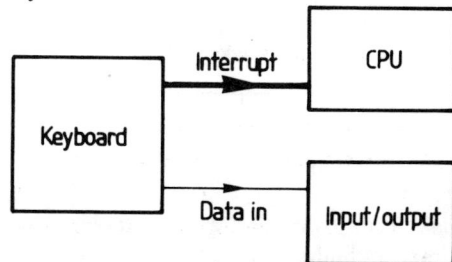

The interrupt signal is generated simultaneously with the setting of a digital input signal, or a data code, when a key is pressed.

(e) Power-up:

It is sensible when a microcomputer is switched on initially to allow a short time, e.g., up to 1 second, to elapse before the main program is initiated. This is to allow the d.c. power supply voltage time to rise and settle. This prevents spurious program operation which can occur when the d.c. rail voltages are unstabilized.

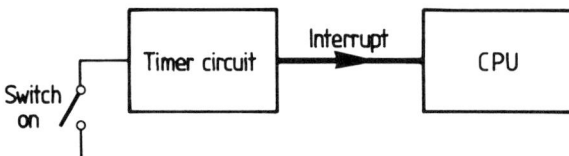

An interrupt is generated which forces the start address of the main program into the program counter. The action of this interrupt normally causes the same restart action as the restart key—see (a) above.

2. Show how it is possible to block, or 'mask out', individual interrupts. In particular, show how higher priority interrupts can be blocked in an interrupt routine.

Answer: The following diagram shows how the CPU gates external interrupt lines with the setting of an internal 'mask' register:

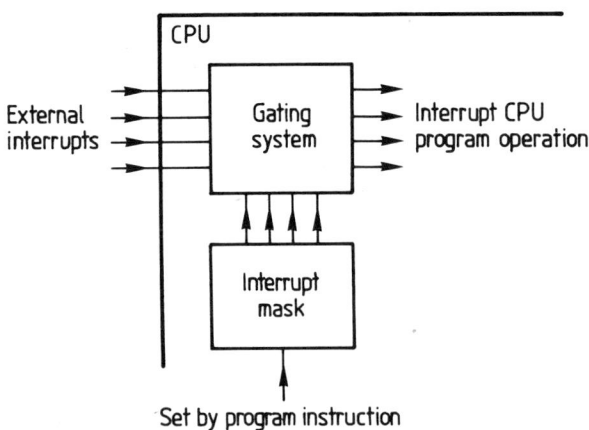

Normally a lower priority interrupt cannot interrupt a higher priority interrupt routine.

However, individual interrupts can be blocked by applying a program instruction which sets appropriate bits in the interrupt mask. Indeed, all interrupts can be blocked if all bits in the mask are set.

It is sensible to mask out all interrupts which are not utilized and which do not therefore possess interrupt routines. Alternatively, an interrupt may be permitted once, but is then blocked. A medium priority interrupt routine may wish to block all interrupts during its execution for timing considerations, and then release other interrupts when it terminates.

Exercises

1. What is an interrupt signal?

2. What is the primary difference between a subroutine and an interrupt routine?

3. Would you choose polling or interrupts for the following devices?
   (a) hard disk;
   (b) temperature signal for data logging purposes;
   (c) position indicator representing objects to be counted—1 pulse every 1 ms

4. What is a nested interrupt?

5. What priorities would you choose if the following interrupt signals are connected to a microcomputer?
   (a) timer (every 1 ms);
   (b) power-up;
   (c) restart pushbutton;
   (d) keyboard

6. Why is a 'power-up' interrupt applied commonly?

7. How can an individual interrupt signal be blocked by software?

8. The following timing diagram shows the timing of the setting of three interrupt signals. Also the timing of the three corresponding interrupt routines are shown discretely, with the

assumption that no other interrupts can occur to give nesting. Assume now that the three interrupts are connected to a single microcomputer in a time-shared nesting arrangement, with interrupt 1 having the highest priority. Identify which interrupt routine runs in each of the timing stages in the bottom diagram (e.g., write a = 3, b = 3, c = 3 if you think that interrupt routine 3 runs during timing stages a, b, and c).

the d.c. supply voltage falls an interrupt routine is entered which provides an orderly shutdown of the microcomputer system, e.g., digital outputs are set to a safe state and the current plant data are dumped from RAM onto floppy disk. Suggest a priority system if the following additional interrupts are applied: an interval timer to provide a real-time clock and an interrupt which indicates that a weight signal is available to be read.

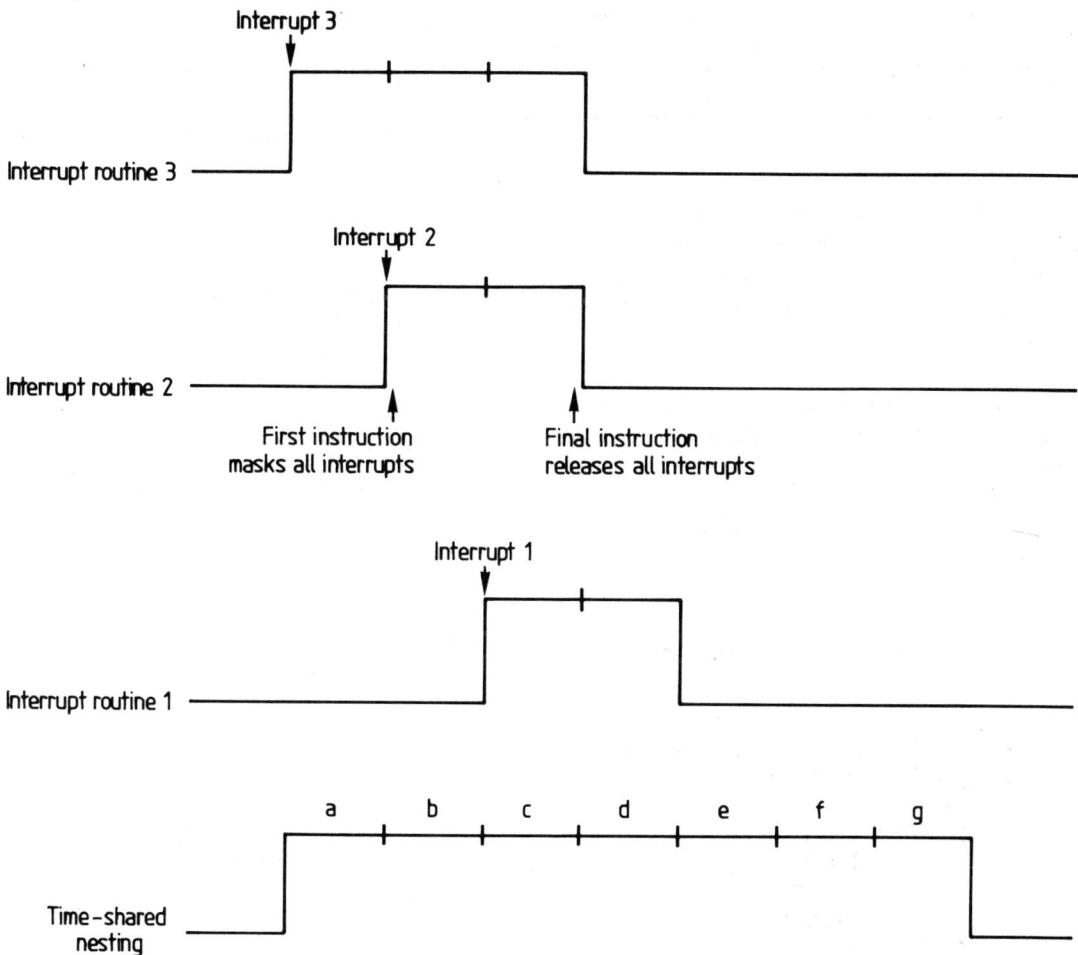

Interrupt 3

Interrupt routine 3

Interrupt 2

Interrupt routine 2

First instruction
masks all interrupts

Final instruction
releases all interrupts

Interrupt 1

Interrupt routine 1

a   b   c   d   e   f   g

Time-shared
nesting

9. What program function is applied commonly with a timer interrupt?

10. A 'power-down' interrupt is required in a particular plant logging system so that when

11. Why are unused interrupts sometimes masked?

4.2 Programming interrupts

We have not yet posed the question: how does the

CPU know the start address of each interrupt routine, i.e., which address overwrites the current contents of the program counter?

The CPU uses reserved memory locations, which are termed *interrupt vectors*, to indicate the start addresses of interrupt routines, as shown in Fig. 4.3.

microcomputer, its vector must also be established. This can only be achieved in the case of a training microcomputer if the memory area which holds the interrupt vectors is in RAM.

Other programming considerations with interrupt routines are:

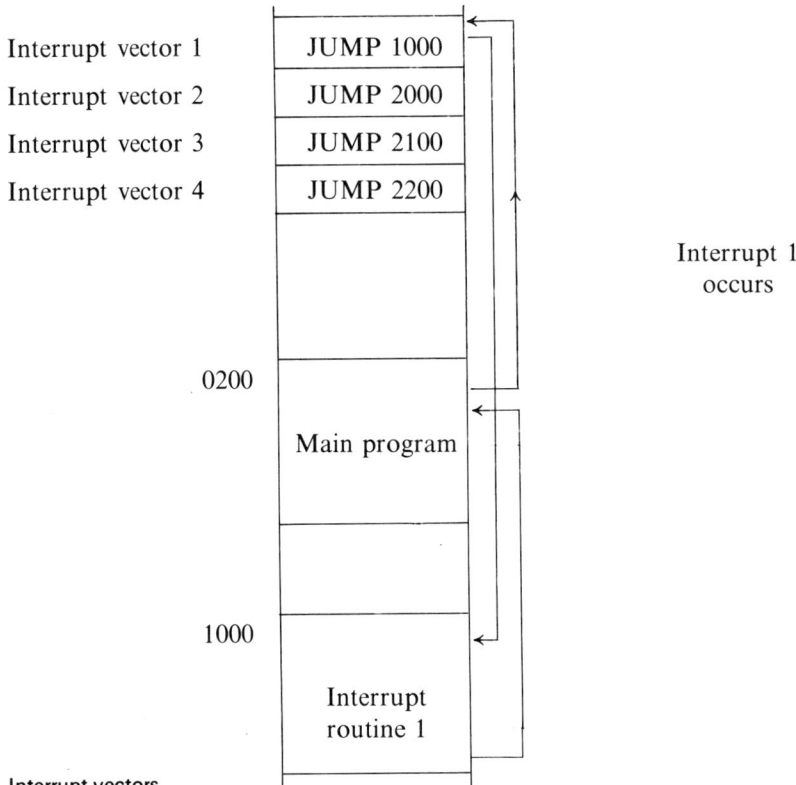

Figure 4.3 Interrupt vectors

When interrupt 1 occurs program control is transferred automatically to a predetermined memory location which holds the interrupt vector. This memory location is fixed by the design of the CPU (e.g., whenever the highest priority interrupt line is set with the Intel 8085, program control is transferred to memory address 0024). The interrupt vector is a JUMP instruction which transfers program control to the start address of the interrupt routine. In some microprocessors the interrupt vector is simply the start address of the interrupt routine and not a JUMP instruction—the jump function is assumed.

It must be remembered therefore that when an interrupt routine is designed and entered into a

(a) Interrupt routines can use subroutines; in fact, all manner of subroutine and interrupt routine nesting is possible, with return addresses being placed on the stack.
(b) Registers must be saved in an interrupt routine to prevent over-writing.
(c) Often it is necessary to reset an interrupt signal in the interrupt routine to allow it to become set again.

Examples

3. List the interrupt vectors for the Intel 8085 microprocessor.

Answer:

Interrupt	Pin legend	Vector address
Interrupt 1	TRAP	0024
Interrupt 2	RST 5.5	002C
Interrupt 3	RST 6.5	0034
Interrupt 4	RST 7.5	003C

Interrupt 1 has the highest priority.

4. List the interrupt mask control instructions for the Intel 8085 microprocessor.

Answer :

EI   Enable interrupt system
DI   Disable interrupt system
SIM   Set interrupt mask with contents of accumulator
RIM   Read interrupt mask into accumulator

5. Write a program for an Intel 8085 microprocessor to generate a continuous tone on a loudspeaker. Additionally, write an interrupt routine which services a pushbutton interrupt signal which is connected to RST 5.5. This routine should illuminate a LED for a short period.

Answer: (a) Memory map:

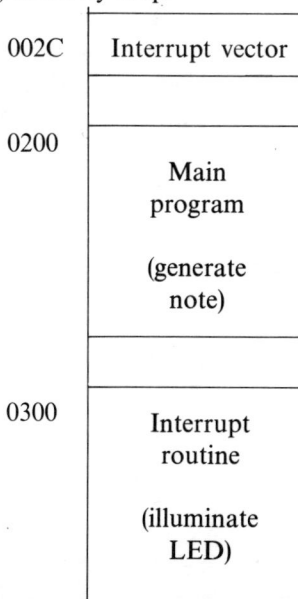

002C	Interrupt vector
0200	Main program (generate note)
0300	Interrupt routine (illuminate LED)

(b) Program:

002C (interrupt vector)
```
      JMP    0300H    Jump to interrupt routine
```

0200 (main program)
```
NOTE: CALL  BUZZ    Subroutine call to generate
                         note
      JMP   NOTE    Repeat
```

0300 (interrupt routine)
```
        PUSH  PSW  ┐ Store A, status register,
        PUSH  B    ┘ B and C on stack
        MVI   A,1  ┐ Output a 1 to LED
        OUT   10H  ┘
        MVI   B,100 ┐
DELAY:  DCR   B     ├ Delay
        JNZ   DELAY ┘
MVI     MVI   A,0  ┐ Output a 0 to LED
        OUT   10H  ┘
        POP   B    ┐ Retrieve A, status register,
        POP   PSW  ┘ B and C off stack
        EI         Re-enable interrupts
        RET        Return to main program
```

The main program generates a continuous sound using the subroutine call to BUZZ, which is not shown. When the pushbutton is pressed the interrupt routine is entered, which lights the LED before returning control to the main program.

Note:

(a) The PUSH and POP operations are necessary in order to preserve the contents of the registers which are used in the interrupt routine. If this is not done the main program is re-entered with these registers over-written.

(b) It may be sensible to segregate all instructions between PUSH B and POP B into a subroutine, as:

```
PUSH   PSW
PUSH   B
CALL   LED    Call subroutine to light LED
POP    B
POP    PSW
EI
RET
```

(c) All interrupts except TRAP are disabled by the CPU during the interrupt routine. Thus the EI instruction must be set at the end of the interrupt routine.

Exercises

12. What is an interrupt vector?

13. What are the two types of interrupt vector?

14. It is possible with a subroutine to push the contents of registers onto the stack within the main program before calling the subroutine. This is an alternative to performing this operation within the subroutine. Why is it not possible to do this within the main program when an interrupt routine is used?

15. What is the function of the EI (enable interrupts) instruction?

16. Can the same subroutine be used by both a main program and an interrupt routine?

17. Write a main program (start address 0300) which flashes a LED at port address 02 and an interrupt routine (start address 0200 and vector at memory address 003C) which increments a count in memory location 1000.

18. Does the intervention of an interrupt routine have any detrimental effects on the execution of the following program sections?
    (a) multiplication section;
    (b) time delay section

19. Can the setting of the TRAP interrupt in an Intel 8085 system cause an interruption of an interrupt routine which is servicing RST 5.5?

20. The interrupt mask for the Intel 8085 is scheduled as follows:

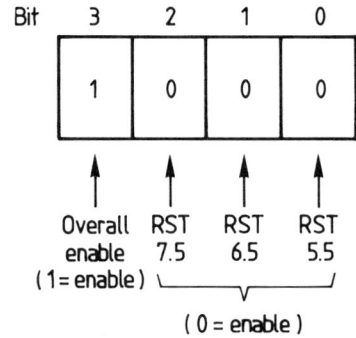

Bit	3	2	1	0
	1	0	0	0

Overall enable (1 = enable) RST 7.5 RST 6.5 RST 5.5

(0 = enable)

All interrupts are shown as enabled.
(a) Which interrupts are enabled by the following?

$$MVI \quad A,0AH$$
$$SIM$$

(b) If the interrupt routine for RST 5.5 ends with

$$MVI \quad A,0EH$$
$$SIM$$
$$EI$$
$$RET$$

which interrupts are enabled subsequently?

21. The interrupt vectors for a particular Intel 8085 system are held in ROM. The 8085 possesses a fifth (lowest priority) interrupt INTR which allows the interrupting peripheral or circuit to supply an instruction (normally a jump to a memory location, which is the start of an interrupt routine) on the data bus. The Zilog Z80 possesses a similar feature. Why is this facility the only means by which an extra interrupt can be added to this particular system?

5 Microelectronic stores

5.1 Memory devices

Within the two general categories of micro-electronic memory (ROM and RAM) there are further subdivisions. The most common types of ROM which are encountered are:
(a) ROM—programmed when the IC is manufactured
(b) PROM—programmed by the user (using a microcomputer 'PROM programmer')
(c) EPROM—erasable PROM (using an UV, or ultraviolet light source)

The two different types of RAM are static RAM and dynamic RAM. Normally RAM circuits are assumed to be static RAM unless specifically defined as dynamic RAM.

All of these devices are normally constructed using MOS technology, which produces high packing density and low power operation.

We will examine examples of ROM, EPROM, static RAM, and dynamic RAM devices so that the reader can interpret manufacturers' data sheets and choose different types of device for particular applications.

Examples

1. Describe a typical ROM device.
Answer: The following diagram shows the pin connections of a 2048×8 (i.e., 2048 words $\times$ 8 bits) ROM:

A7	1	24	V_{CC}
A6	2	23	A8
A5	3	22	A9
A4	4	21	CS3
A3	5	20	CS1
A2	6	2048 × 8 ROM 19	A10
A1	7	18	CS2
A0	8	17	D7
D0	9	16	D6
D1	10	15	D5
D2	11	14	D4
GND	12	13	D3

Notice the following features:
(a) Eleven address lines give 2^{11} ($=2048$) memory locations.
(b) Eight data lines give byte (eight-bit) storage.
(c) D.C. supply lines ($+5\,V$ and $0\,V$)—V_{CC} and GND.
(d) Three chip selects—these inputs are programmable when the device is manufactured at the masking stage. Thus any bit pattern can be specified on these signal lines to invoke the normal chip select function (activate the chip).

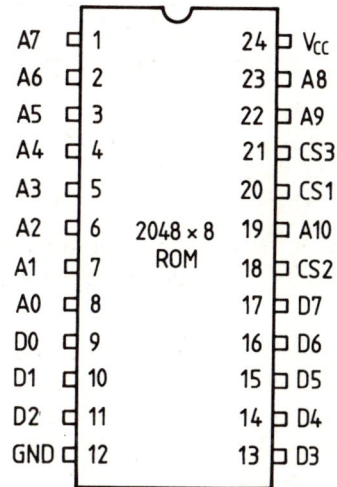

This device is offered by several manufacturers with a virtually identical specification, e.g., the Intel 8316A and the Synetek 2316A (slightly different pin layout). Notice that the last two digits 16 normally identify the memory size (16K bits).

All input and output signals are 'TTL compatible', i.e., possess electrical characteristics (notably $+5\,V$ and $0\,V$ signal levels) which enable connection to TTL and other MOS circuits.

A typical specification is:

Storage capacity	16K bits (2048×8)
Access time	500 ns ($0.5\ \mu s$)
Power consumption	0.5 W (W = watt)
Price	£1·00

2. Describe a typical EPROM device.
Answer: The following diagram shows the pin connections of a 2048×8 EPROM, i.e., the same memory capacity as Example 1:

```
         ┌────────┬─────────┐
A7  ⊏ 1 │        │ 24 ⊐ V_CC
A6  ⊏ 2 │        │ 23 ⊐ A8
A5  ⊏ 3 │2048 × 8│ 22 ⊐ A9
A4  ⊏ 4 │EP ROM  │ 21 ⊐ V_PP
A3  ⊏ 5 │        │ 20 ⊐ CS̄
A2  ⊏ 6 │        │ 19 ⊐ A10
A1  ⊏ 7 │        │ 18 ⊐ PD/PGM
A0  ⊏ 8 │Erasing │ 17 ⊐ D7
D0  ⊏ 9 │window  │ 16 ⊐ D6
D1  ⊏ 10│        │ 15 ⊐ D5
D2  ⊏ 11│        │ 14 ⊐ D4
GND ⊏ 12│        │ 13 ⊐ D3
         └────────┴─────────┘
```

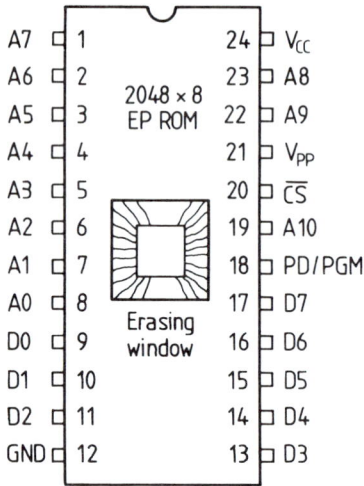

Notice the following features:
(a) Eleven address lines give 2^{11} ($= 2048$) memory locations.
(b) Eight data lines give byte (eight-bit) storage.
(c) Two d.c. supply lines ($+ 5$ V and 0 V)—V_{CC} and GND.
(d) One chip select (notice that $\overline{CS}$ implies that inverse logic is used, i.e., the signal is set when it is at logic 0 or 0 V).
(e) Two extra pins compared with the ROM device as follows:
PD/PGM is the programming signal which is pulsed when the device is being programmed. When the device is used normally, this signal can be used to place the chip into the 'power-down' state, i.e., when data are not being read, a 1 on this signal line reduces the power dissipation of the device.
V_{pp} is only used during the programming procedure when it is held at a high voltage level ($+24$ V). During normal operation it is connected to V_{CC}.
A transparent window is built into the package to facilitate the erasure operation. This window should be covered (e.g., by adhesive paper or plastic tape) during normal operation to prevent accidental erasure.
Again, several manufacturers offer this device, which is defined as a 2716 ($16 = 16$K bits). When supplied blank, or after erasure, all bits are set to 1. A typical specification is:

Storage capacity	16K bits (2048×8)
Access time	500 ns (0.5 μs)
Power dissipation	1.0 W
Price	£4-00

3. Describe a typical static RAM device.
Answer: The following diagram shows the pin connections of a 1024×4 static RAM:

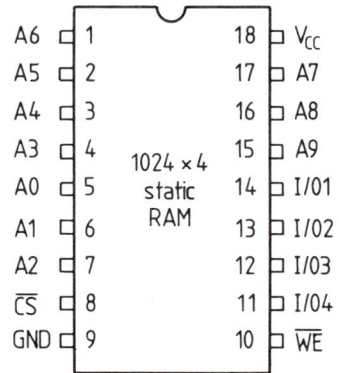

```
         ┌────────┬─────────┐
A6  ⊏ 1 │        │ 18 ⊐ V_CC
A5  ⊏ 2 │        │ 17 ⊐ A7
A4  ⊏ 3 │        │ 16 ⊐ A8
A3  ⊏ 4 │1024 × 4│ 15 ⊐ A9
A0  ⊏ 5 │static  │ 14 ⊐ I/O1
A1  ⊏ 6 │RAM     │ 13 ⊐ I/O2
A2  ⊏ 7 │        │ 12 ⊐ I/O3
CS̄  ⊏ 8 │        │ 11 ⊐ I/O4
GND ⊏ 9 │        │ 10 ⊐ WĒ
         └────────┴─────────┘
```

Notice the following features:
(a) Ten address lines give 2^{10} ($= 1024$) memory locations.
(b) Four data lines give nibble (four-bit) storage.
(c) Two d.c. supply lines ($+ 5$ V and 0 V)—V_{CC} and GND.
(d) One chip select.
(e) One write enable ($\overline{WE}$ is inverse logic).
The device is four-bit only; therefore two ICs must be connected onto the two halves of the data bus to give byte storage.
The features which are discernible immediately as additional to ROM requirements are those associated with the write *and* read operations. viz.:

write enable, to distinguish between read and write operations, and bidirectional data flow on the I/O pins

Clearly this makes the device more complex than ROM since additional circuitry is built into the chip to handle write operations. Therefore the packing density is reduced. For this reason, static RAM is generally packaged in four-bit (occasionally one-bit) devices.
An essential consideration with RAM is its volatility, i.e., it loses its stored bit pattern (program

and data) when d.c. power is removed. Similarly, bits are set in an unpredictable manner when d.c. power is applied.

This device is described as a 2114 (4 = 4K bits) and is offered by several manufacturers. A typical specification is:

Storage capacity	4K bits (1024 × 4)
Access time	300 ns
Power dissipation	1.0 W
Price	£2-50

4. Describe a typical dynamic RAM device.

Answer: The following diagram shows the pin connections of a 4096 × 1 dynamic RAM, i.e., the same memory capacity as Example 3:

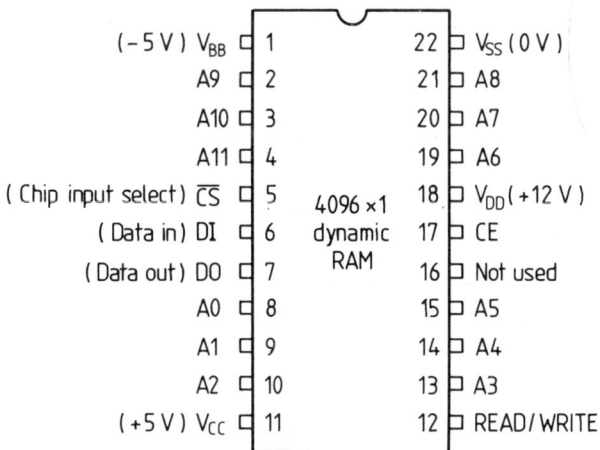

```
         (-5 V) V_BB ⊏ 1      ⌒    22 ⊐ V_SS (0 V)
              A9 ⊏ 2           21 ⊐ A8
             A10 ⊏ 3           20 ⊐ A7
             A11 ⊏ 4           19 ⊐ A6
(Chip input select) C̄S̄ ⊏ 5  4096 ×1   18 ⊐ V_DD (+12 V)
        (Data in) DI ⊏ 6  dynamic  17 ⊐ CE
       (Data out) DO ⊏ 7    RAM    16 ⊐ Not used
              A0 ⊏ 8           15 ⊐ A5
              A1 ⊏ 9           14 ⊐ A4
              A2 ⊏ 10          13 ⊐ A3
       (+5 V) V_CC ⊏ 11        12 ⊐ READ/WRITE
```

Notice the following features:
(a) Twelve address lines give 2^{12} ($= 4096$) memory locations.
(b) One data line for each of data input and output (clearly these must be combined externally before connection is made to one of the data bus lines).
(c) Four d.c. power supply lines ($+12\,V$, $+5\,V$, $-5\,V$, $0\,V$).
(d) Two chip selects—CE and $\overline{CS}$.
(e) One read/write.

The only significant difference between this IC and the previous static RAM device (apart from the addition of $+12\,V$ and $-5\,V$ supply lines) is the application of the refresh facility. Dynamic RAM must be 'refreshed' more frequently than once every 2 ms in order to prevent loss of data. The refreshing action is accomplished by simply reading sequentially the 64 locations designated by the address lines A0 to A5. Thus an external circuit must set all 64 bit patterns on these six address lines within 2 ms of the previous refresh.

Dynamic RAM possesses the following advantages over static RAM:

> smaller (higher packing density), lower power, faster, cheaper

However, it does require a refresh circuit. It is used predominantly for large-capacity memory systems.

Several manufacturers, e.g., Intel and Mitsubishi, offer this device, which is termed a 2107. A typical specification is:

Storage capacity	4K bits (4096 × 1)
Access time	200 ns
Power dissipation	0.3 W
Cost	£1-50

A novel technique for size reduction is applied with some dynamic RAM devices, e.g., the 16K-bit (16384 × 1) 4116. Only half of the total number of 14 address lines are connected to the IC, as shown at the top of the next page.

The row address (A0 to A6) is first presented on the seven address lines together with the RAS signal. Approximately 100 ns later the column address (A7 to A13) is set on the same address lines together with the CAS signal. This time-multiplexing control circuit is constructed externally to the IC. Refresh is achieved by setting the row address lines A0 to A6 (with RAS therefore) faster than every 2 ms.

Exercises

1. Name:
   (a) three different types of read-only memory and
   (b) two different types of read/write memory.

2. What does the description 'TTL compatible' mean?

3. List the essential pin functions of a 1024 × 8 ROM.

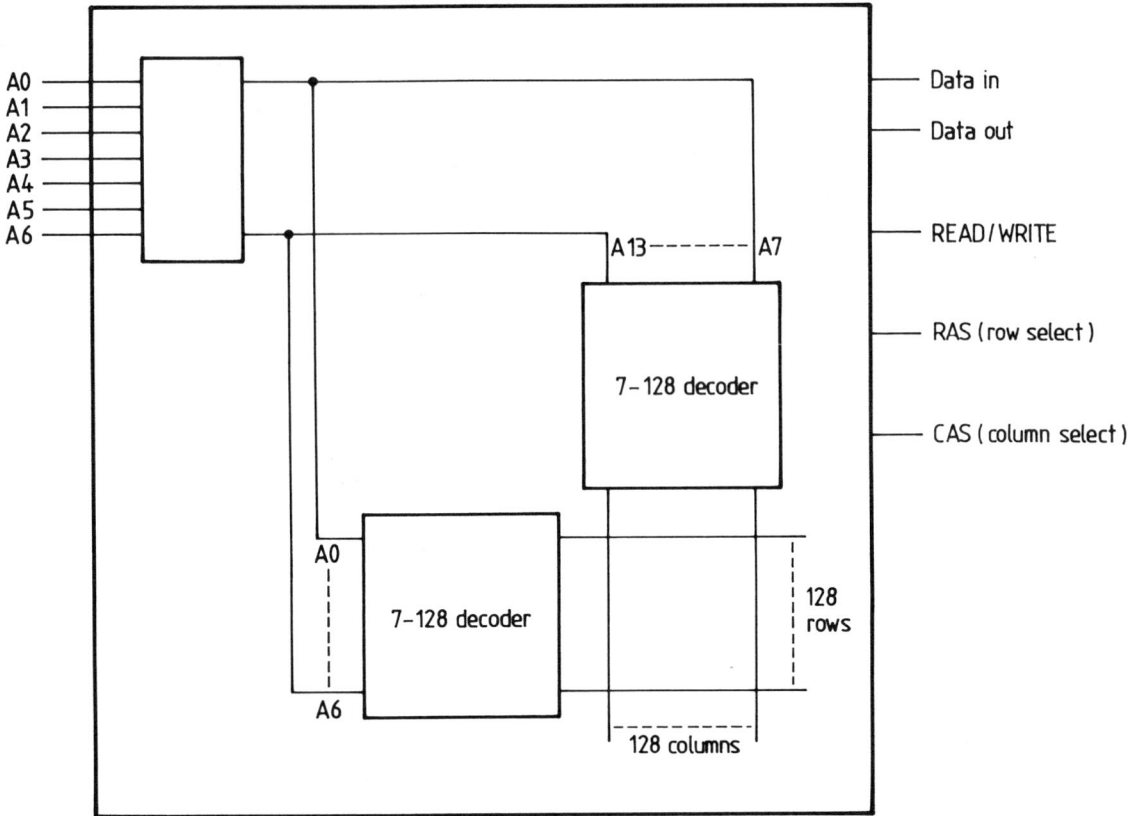

4. What is a 2716?

5. What is a 'refreshing' dynamic RAM?

6. Which technology is used in the manufacture of most ROM and RAM devices—TTL, MOS, or CMOS?

7. What is a typical data read time for ROM?

8. What does the bar in the symbol $\overline{CS}$ indicate?

9. (a) How is an EPROM device erased?
   (b) What are the settings of all bits after erasure?
   (c) What measures should be applied to the erasure window after the device is programmed?

10. Why is it not sensible to build a 128K-byte ROM chip for connection to an eight-bit microprocessor?

11. What is 'nibble' storage?

12. One-bit dynamic RAM devices possess one pin for data in and one pin for data out. Why is this a disadvantage?

13. A fully developed program for a plant logging and control microcomputer system is placed in ROM. Why do you think that some RAM is also necessary?

14. The device at the top of the next page combines a memory circuit and an input/output port (four bits only). What type of memory is used and what is its capacity?

15. What difference do you think exists between a 2708 and a 2716?

16. Why do you think that the 2316 ROM chip is precisely pin-compatible with the 2716?

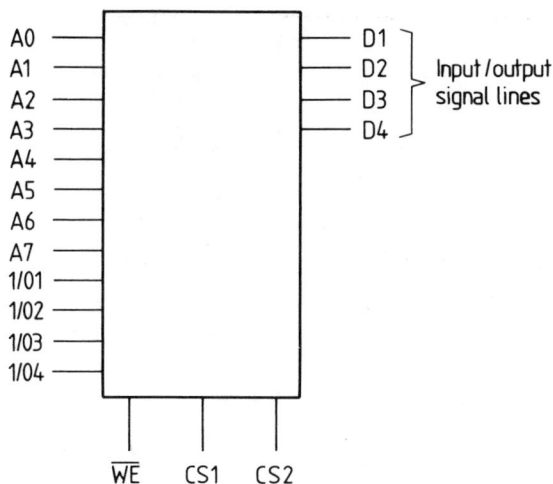

A0 — D1
A1 — D2 ⎫ Input/output
A2 — D3 ⎬ signal lines
A3 — D4 ⎭
A4
A5
A6
A7
1/01
1/02
1/03
1/04

$\overline{WE}$ CS1 CS2

17. State four advantages of dynamic RAM over static RAM for a large memory system.

18. Which memory device is most likely to be used in a high-volume microcomputer application, e.g., to store a video game program?

19. What time-multiplexing function is necessary with some dynamic RAM devices? What advantage does it give?

20. Complete the following table:

Characteristic	Device			
	ROM 2048 × 8 (2316)	EPROM 2048 × 8 (2716)	Dynamic RAM 1024 × 4 (2114)	Static RAM 4096 × 1 (2107)
Number of bits				
Read speed (ns)				
Power consumption (W)				
Cost (£)				
Cost/1K bits (£)				

5.2 Memory systems

We have already met the concept of data bus sharing by two RAM devices which are only four bits wide. The four least significant data lines feed one device and the four most significant data lines feed the other device, as shown in Fig. 5.1.

The Chip Select and Read/Write signals feed both ICs. Thus both chips are selected and operate in unison. Similarly, byte storage systems can be built up for one-bit RAM devices by placing eight ICs in parallel on the data bus, with each chip handling just one of the data lines.

The important design criterion when generating Chip Select signals for an assembly of memory devices is that only one Chip Select signal should be set at any time. Therefore only one memory device responds to an address on the address bus and attempts to read data from, or write data to, the data bus. An address decoder chip (or circuit) performs this function. Such a device is shown in Fig. 5.2.

This device was described in Sec. 2.2 (Fig. 2.4) where it was used to generate one of four discrete output signals for a binary code on the two input signals. The same function is performed in this application. Each of the output signals feeds to the CS (chip select) pin of a different memory device— ROM or RAM. Table 5.1 shows that only one Chip Select signal is set for any bit combination on the two address lines A_n and A_{n+1}.

Table 5.1 Truth table for 2 to 4 address decoder IC

A_{n+1}	A_n	CS4	CS3	CS2	CS1
0	0	0	0	0	1
0	1	0	0	1	0
1	0	0	1	0	0
1	1	1	0	0	0

A 3 to 8 decoder chip may be necessary if there are more than four memory devices in the system.

When many memory and input/output ICs are connected onto the address and data busses in a microcomputer system, it may be necessary to instal bus drivers. Simply, these devices provide electrical buffering and enable the bus signals to drive large IC configurations. A single IC can provide this facility for eight signals, e.g., the whole of the data bus or one half of the address bus, as shown in Fig. 5.3.

This feature is required more frequently in a multi-board configuration. This occurs in many personal or business microcomputer systems; Fig. 5.4 shows a typical configuration.

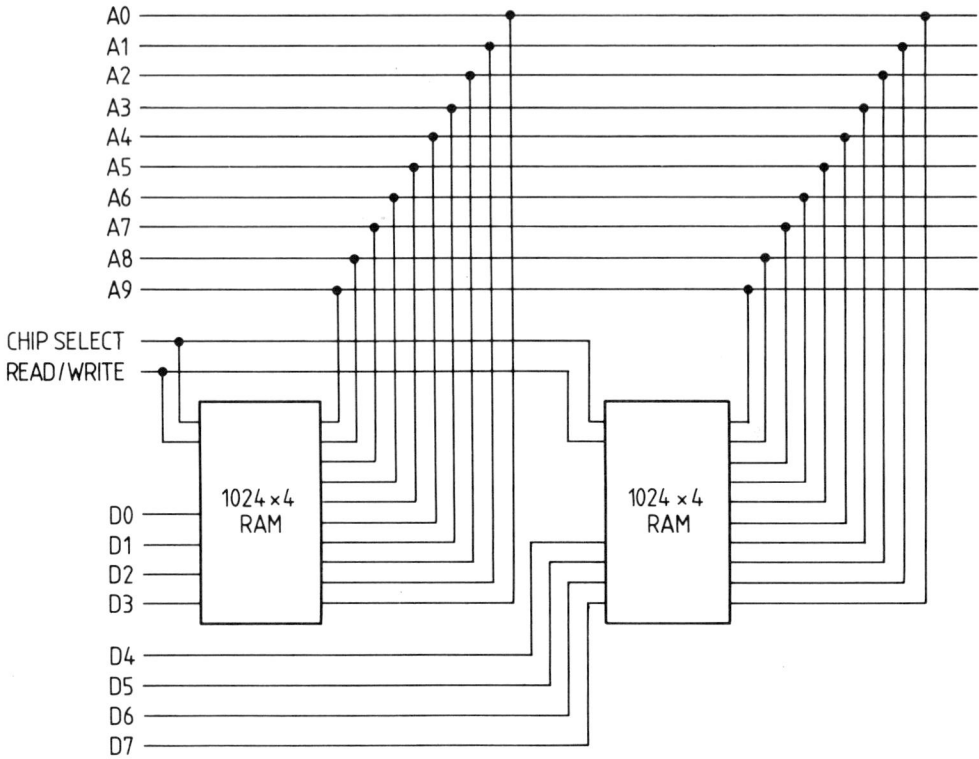

Figure 5.1 A 1K-byte RAM (2 off 1024×4 ICs)

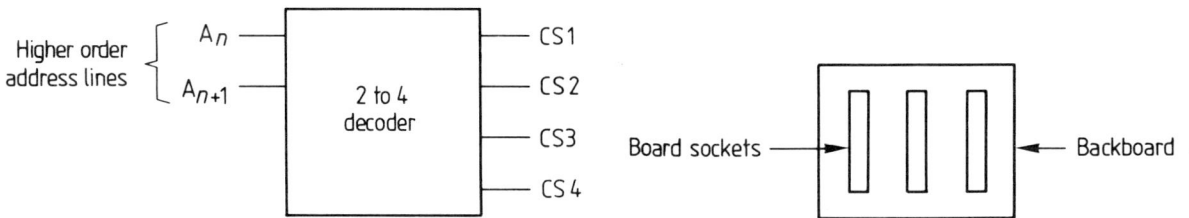

Figure 5.2 A 2 to 4 decoder IC

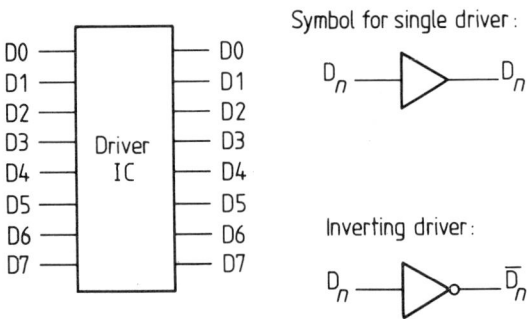

Figure 5.3 Drivers (for data bus)

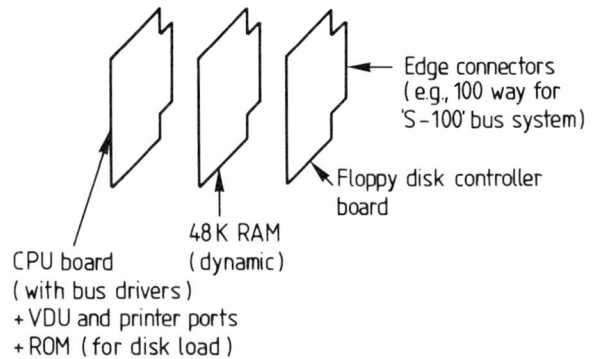

Figure 5.4 Typical multi-board configuration

Examples

5. Examine the following memory circuit:

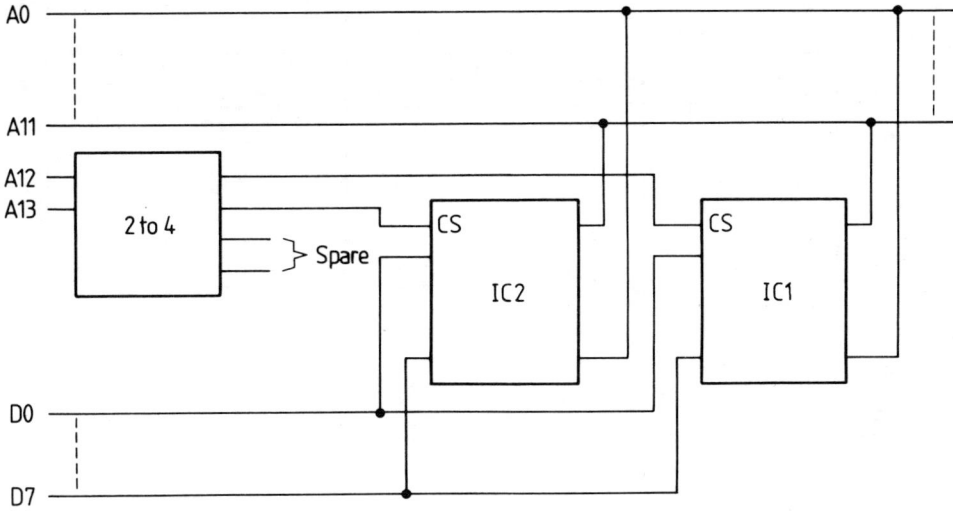

Answer the following:
   (a) What are the memory chips IC1 and IC2?
   (b) How many locations do they possess?
   (c) What is the start address of each chip?
   (d) Draw a memory map for the configuration.

Answer:
(a) IC1 and IC2 are ROM (no Read/Write signal).
(b) Each possesses 4K locations since 12 address
     lines are used:

$$2^{12} = 4K$$

Therefore, each device is 4096×8 (eight data lines
are connected).
(c) Start address of IC1:

Block address

A15	A14	A13	A12	A11	A10	A9	A8
0	0	0	0	0	0	0	0

Hex: 0   0

A7	A6	A5	A4	A3	A2	A1	A0
0	0	0	0	0	0	0	0

Hex: 0   0

Therefore, the start address of IC1 is *hex, 0000*.
Start address of IC2:

Block address

A15	A14	A13	A12	A11	A10	A9	A8
0	0	0	1	0	0	0	0

Hex: 1   0

A7	A6	A5	A4	A3	A2	A1	A0
0	0	0	0	0	0	0	0

Hex: 0   0

Therefore, the start address of IC2 is *hex. 1000*.
(d) Memory map:

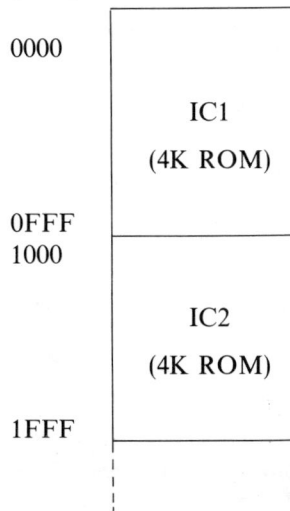

6. Examine the following memory circuit:

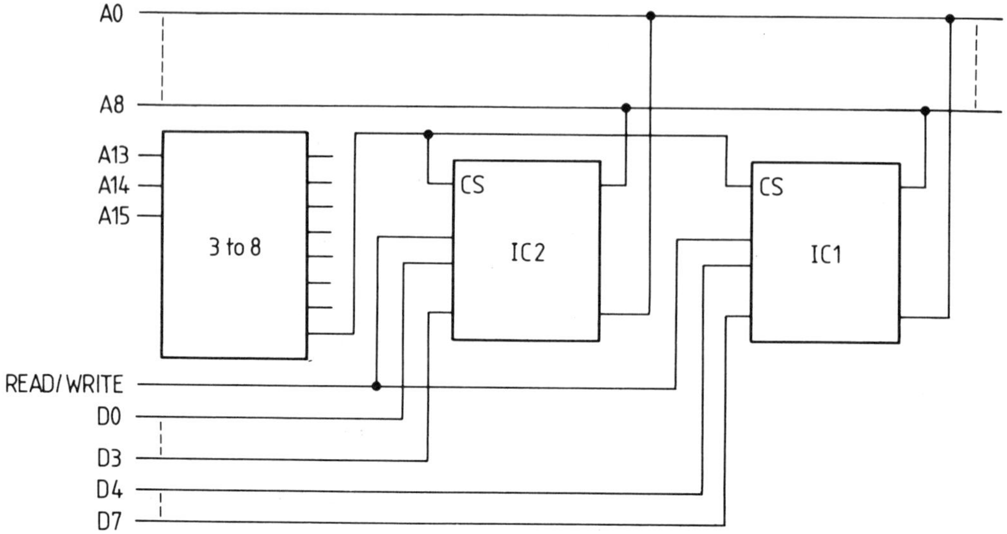

Answer the following:
(a) What are the memory chips IC1 and IC2?
(b) How many memory locations do they possess?
(c) What is the start address of each chip?
(d) Draw a memory map for the configuration.

Answer:

(a) IC1 and IC2 are RAM (Read/Write signal is connected).

(b) Each possesses 512 locations since nine address lines are used:

$$2^9 = 512$$

(c) Both possess the same start address (they share the same chip select):

Block address

A15	A14	A13	A12	A11	A10	A9	A8
1	1	1	0	0	0	0	0

Hex: E   0

A7	A6	A5	A4	A3	A2	A1	A0
0	0	0	0	0	0	0	0

      0   0

Notice that each of A13, A14, and A15 must be set to 1 to set the last output on the 3 to 8 decoder chip. Therefore, the start address of the IC1 and IC2 pair is *hex. E000*.

(d) Memory map:

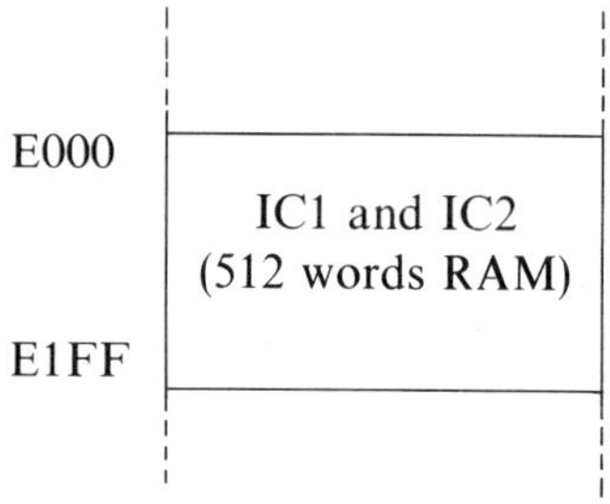

The reader may like to confirm that the last address in RAM is E1FF.

7. Draw the circuit symbol and truth table for a 3 to 8 decoder which is used for 'block addressing'.

Answer: Circuit symbol:

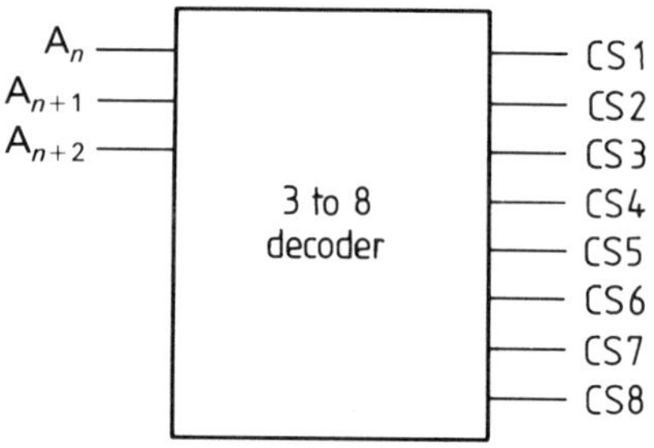

Truth table:

A_{n+2}	A_{n+1}	A_n	CS8	CS7	CS6	CS5	CS4	CS3	CS2	CS1
0	0	0	0	0	0	0	0	0	0	1
0	0	1	0	0	0	0	0	0	1	0
0	1	0	0	0	0	0	0	1	0	0
0	1	1	0	0	0	0	1	0	0	0
1	0	0	0	0	0	1	0	0	0	0
1	0	1	0	0	1	0	0	0	0	0
1	1	0	0	1	0	0	0	0	0	0
1	1	1	1	0	0	0	0	0	0	0

8. A microcomputer system includes:
   (a) 1K ROM (1024 × 8 IC);
   (b) 512 words RAM (2 off 512 × 4 ICs);
   (c) input/output IC;
   (d) 2 to 4 decoder IC

   The input/output is 'memory mapped', i.e., it is connected into the circuit in the same manner as a memory device and is accessed using the same program instructions (e.g., LDA, STA in place of IN, OUT).

   Draw a circuit which performs these functions.

Answer:

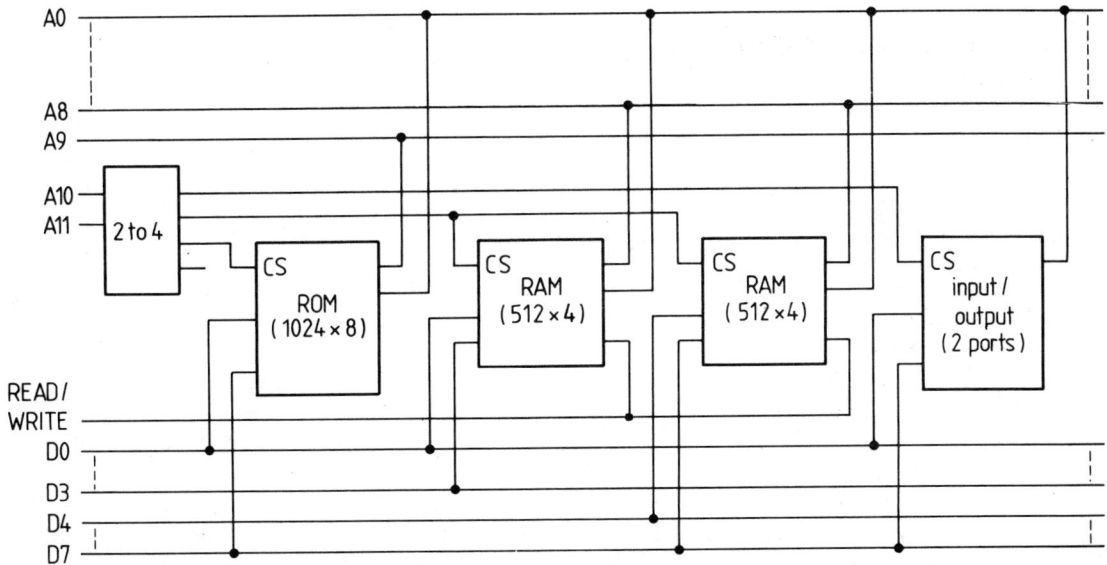

Notice that ten address lines are connected to ROM, nine address lines are connected to RAM, and one address line is connected to the input/output IC (to select port A or port B).

Exercises

21. What is the name of the IC which generates chip select signals?

22. What bit pattern must be set on the three inputs to a 3 to 8 decoder IC to set the penultimate (last-but-one) output signal to 1?

23. What is a bus driver?

24. Sketch a circuit which creates 16K bytes of RAM memory using 8 off 16384 × 1 RAM ICs.

25. Examine the circuit in Example 6. A memory test program, which writes eight bits to each RAM location and then reads back the eight bits, indicates storage errors in all locations. Which IC is faulty?

26. Examine the circuit in Example 8. What are the addresses of:
    (a) first location in ROM;
    (b) first location in RAM;
    (c) the two input/output ports

27. The following circuit shows the use of a 3 to 8 decoder IC to provide chip select signals for several memory devices within a microcomputer. What are the start and end addresses of ROM3?

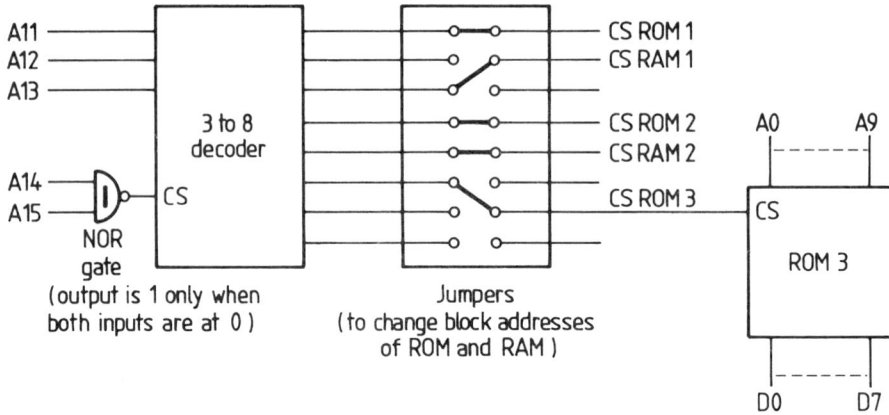

A11 —— 3 to 8 decoder —— CS ROM 1
A12 —— CS RAM 1
A13 ——

A14 —— NOR gate —— CS
A15 ——

CS ROM 2
CS RAM 2
CS ROM 3

A0   A9

CS
ROM 3

D0   D7

NOR gate
(output is 1 only when both inputs are at 0)

Jumpers
(to change block addresses of ROM and RAM)

Notice that the decoder IC itself possesses a chip select function.

28. Examine the circuit in Example 5. Why is it not possible to use one of the two spare outputs from the decoder chip as a Chip Select signal to an 8192×8 ROM chip?

29. Identify any errors in the following diagram:

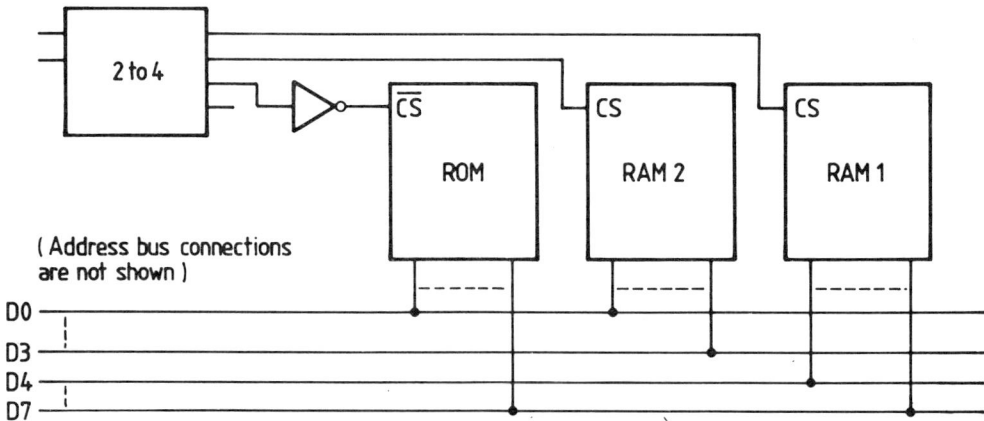

2 to 4

CS
ROM

CS
RAM 2

CS
RAM 1

(Address bus connections are not shown)

D0
D3
D4
D7

(b) 2 off 2114 RAM (base address 4000);
(c) 2316 ROM (base address 8000);
(d) 2 off 74LS373 parallel input/output ports (see Sec. 2.2, Example 11); 1 connected as an output port (address 20) and the other connected as an input port (address 21);
(e) 2 off 2 to 4 decoders;
(f) inverters (as required)

30. Draw the truth table for a 4 to 10 decoder. Notice that the last six code combinations are not used.

31. Draw a detailed circuit diagram for a complete microcomputer system which possesses the following:
    (a) microprocessor—A0 to A15, D0 to D7, $\overline{\text{WRITE}}$, clock ϕ, DC connections, plus other control signals;

32. The following diagram shows a microcomputer memory system:
    Now answer the following:
    (a) Identify chips 1 to 8, giving the memory capacity where appropriate.
    (b) Draw a memory map for the system (it is recommended that you write down all address line settings for each memory device).
    (c) Which signals from the circuit would you

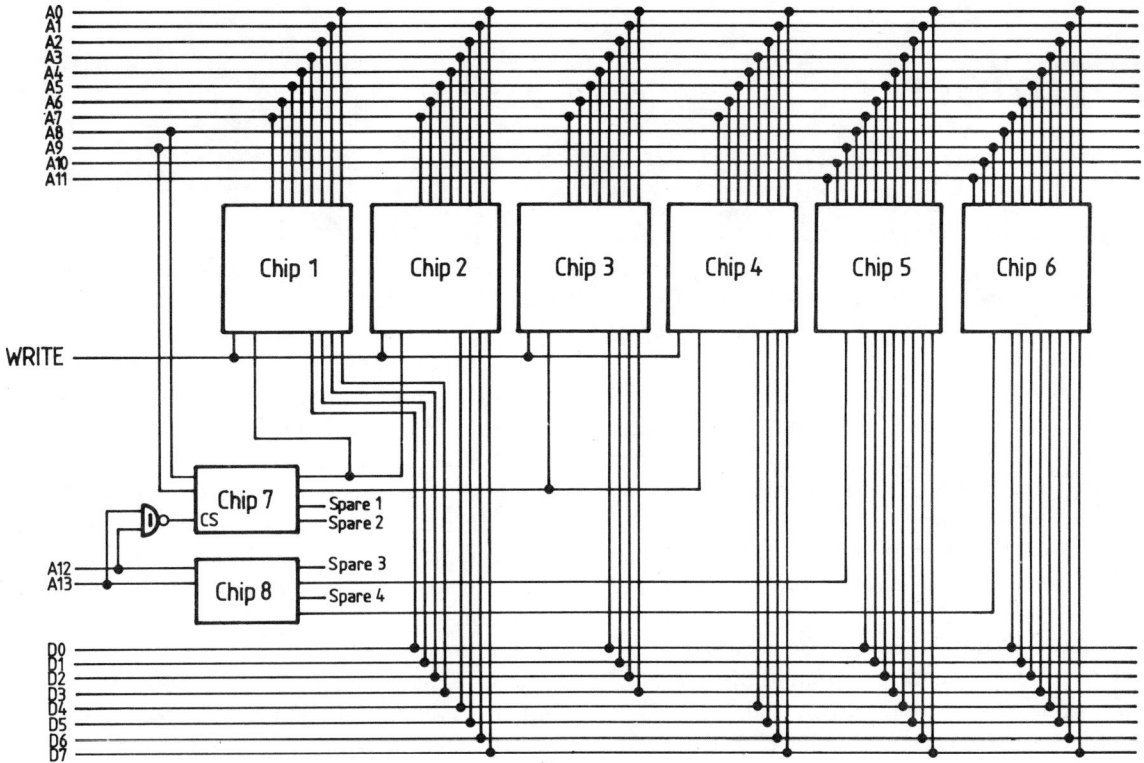

need to connect to an additional 2K ROM which is to have an address range starting at hex. 2000?

(d) Why is the NOR gate necessary? Both inputs to the NOR gate must be zero to generate the chip select (CS) for chip 7.

6 Timers

A microcomputer program can implement time delays by simple delay loops, i.e., set a loop count which is decremented successively to zero. Delays are often necessary when input/output polling is performed.

An alternative technique involves the use of an external counter circuit. The program sends a count to the device, which counts down to zero and then sets an output signal. This signal can be used to interrupt the machine.

The advantages of an external counter circuit are:
(a) The program can perform other duties during the delay.
(b) A more accurate delay can be achieved.

The counter IC is connected onto the bus systems as if it is an input/output device. Indeed, it often forms part of a parallel input/output chip. Figure 6.1 shows the principle of operation.

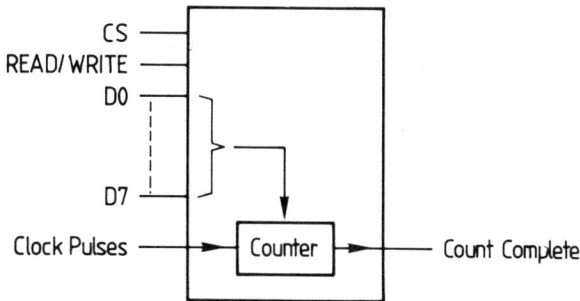

Figure 6.1 Interval timer

The connection signals are as follows:
(a) CS (Chip Select). This is generated by a decoder chip from selected address lines in the usual manner as for memory and input/output ICs.
(b) READ/WRITE. The read function, which is not used normally, is available to enable software to read the current value in the counter.
(c) D0–D7. The number which is to be counted down enters on the data bus connections, with READ/WRITE set to write.

(d) Clock Pulses. These are set to a precise frequency to enable accurate time intervals to be generated; generally the CPU clock ϕ, or a signal which is derived from it, is used.
(e) Count Complete. This signal indicates the end of the countdown procedure and can be read by the CPU; alternatively, it can interrupt the CPU.

Often more than one counter (up to three) is constructed on an interval timer chip. Additionally, it is common for a parallel input/output IC to offer an interval timer circuit as part of its overall function.

The interval timer circuit can be used for the following purposes:
(a) Interval timer, i.e., generate a precise time delay.
(b) Regular interrupt pulses, e.g., every 10 ms, to enable an interrupt routine to maintain a time-of-day clock. In this case the counter is reset automatically after each timed interval is completed so that the countdown procedure recommences.
(c) Event counter, if the clock pulses are external signals which it is required to count.

Examples

1. Show how the Intel 8155 interval timer chip (which includes 256×8 RAM plus 3 parallel input/output ports) can be used to generate a time delay of 1 ms.
Answer: (see figure top of next page)

The following connections are not shown for simplicity:
(a) address lines;
(b) input/output ports

A 4 MHz crystal input to the 8085 CPU is divided within the CPU to produce a 2 MHz clock signal CLK(OUT). If this signal (0.5 μs interval) is used to decrement the count within the interval timer IC,

46

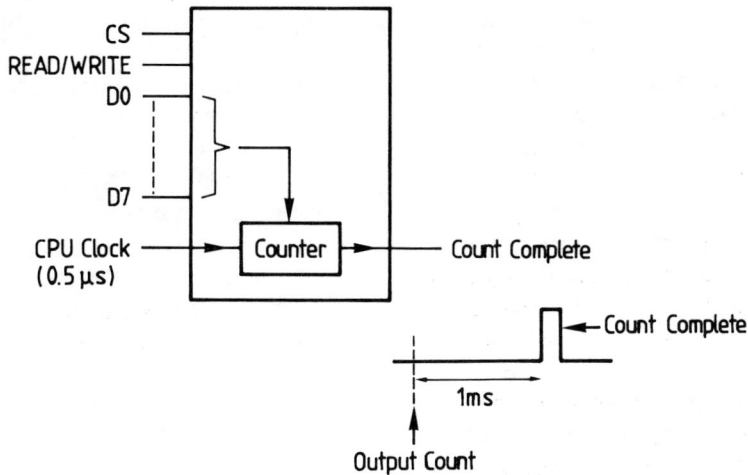

then a 1 ms interval can be computed as follows:

Count $\times 0.5 \; \mu s \quad = 1 \; ms$

Therefore, $count = \dfrac{10^{-3}}{0.5 \times 10^{-6}}$

$= 2000$ (or hex. 07E0)

The count is output as a 14-bit number; an additional two bits indicate the timer mode (e.g., 10 = single pulse output, 11 = automatic reload of count to give repetitive pulses). Thus:

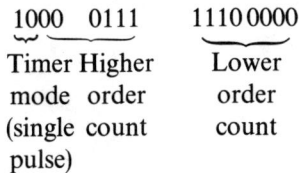

1000 0111	1110 0000
Timer Higher mode order (single count pulse)	Lower order count

must be sent to the timer.

If the addresses on the chip are:

Control register $= 10$
Count (low order)$| = 14$
Count (high order) $= 15$

(Addresses 11, 12, and 13 are ports A, B, and C)

then a program which activates the timer to produce a Count Complete signal after 1 ms is:

MVI	A,E0H	}	Output low order half of
OUT	14H		count (E0)
MVI	A,87H	}	Output high order half of
OUT	15H		count (07) + timer mode
MVI	A,C0H	}	Output control bits to
OUT	10H		activate timer

2. Demonstrate how a repetitive 1 ms pulse can be generated by an interval timer to produce a 'real-time clock' interrupt.

Answer:

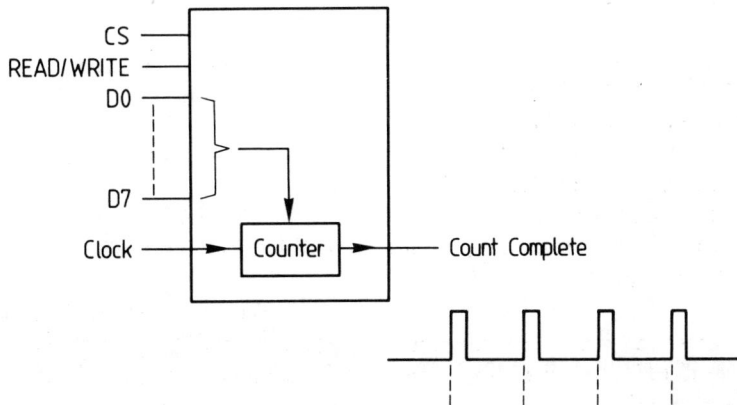

The two-bit timer mode field which is sent to initiate the interval timer in Example 1 must be changed from 10 to 11 to cause automatic reset of the count when each Count Complete signal is generated.

If the Count Complete is connected as an interrupt signal to the CPU, the interrupt routine which is called every 1 ms can update a time-of-day clock which it holds in memory. Thus, every 100 interrupts a 'tenths of seconds' count is incremented by 1; when this number reaches 10 a 'seconds' count is incremented; etc. for 'tens of seconds' and then minutes and hours.

This time-of-day clock can be used to:
(a) Add the time to a message which is presented to the operator on a VDU or printer, e.g.,

13.26 PLANT STEAM FLOW LOW ALARM

(b) Call a program on a regular basis, e.g., scan a keyboard every 100 ms or scan plant analogue signals every second.
(c) Call a program at a particular time of day, e.g., at 09.00 display a work schedule for the day or at 14.00 print a shift summary.

3. Demonstrate how an interval timer IC can be used as an event counter.
Answer:

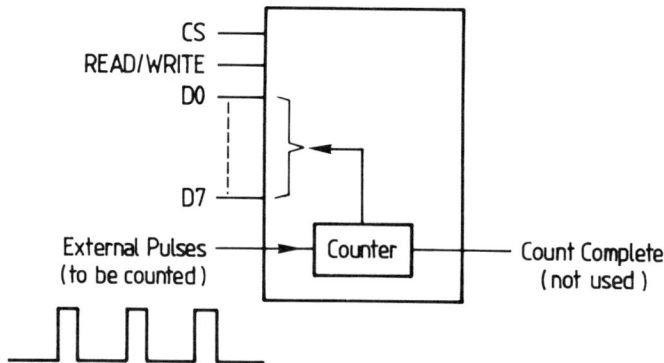

In this arrangement the clock signal from the CPU is replaced by an external stream of pulses. Also, the counter is not loaded with a count from the CPU. Instead, the counter, which is set to increment and not decrement (as in previous examples), is read back into the CPU to determine the number of external pulses which occur. The counter can be

reset to zero by the CPU to enable a new count to be initiated.

Notice that the Intel 8155 interval timer IC cannot be set into an increment mode to perform this event counting function. However, an alternative chip, the 8253, which possesses three counters, can be used in the increment mode.

The type of external signal may be:
(a) items passing a position detector, e.g., boxes on a conveyor belt intercepting a light beam to trigger a photodetector;
(b) pulses indicating batches of material, e.g., hopper gate operation, lorry loaded, etc., so that a total weight can be computed

Exercises

1. State three applications of a counter-timer chip.

2. The Count Complete signal is generated when an interval timer countdown finishes. State two software methods of applying this signal to activate a program response, e.g., to initiate a numerical display program.

3. Why is it better to use an interval timer rather than a program delay loop in order to generate a time delay?

4. Why is the CPU clock, or a derivative of it, normally connected to an interval timer chip?

5. When is a counter-timer set into an increment rather than a decrement mode?

6. Why must an eight-bit microprocessor

implement three output operations in order to set an interval timer?

7. State possible uses of a regular 10 ms interrupt from a counter-timer.

8. What count (in hex.) must be sent to the interval timer chip in Example 1 to generate a time delay of 5 ms?

9. There are often two clocks operating within a microcomputer system which includes an interval timer to assist its keyboard scanning function. What are they?

10. Sketch a diagram which shows how the following circuit can be connected to a micro-computer counter-timer:

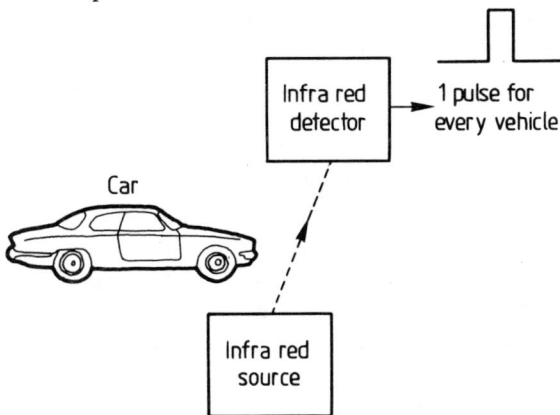

11. It is required to connect the following triple-counter IC (Intel 8253) into a microcomputer configuration such that counters 0, 1, and 2 have addresses hex. 20, 21, and 22 respectively. A 2 to 4 decoder IC is available. Sketch the circuit and address bus connections which are required to the bottom left-hand three pins.

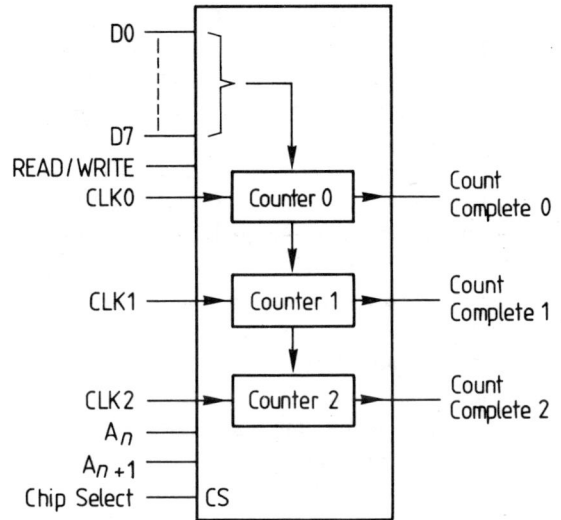

7 Programming examples

There are three 'levels' of programming:

(a) *Machine code*, i.e., write the program in binary (or its hex. equivalent). This is a laborious procedure and requires the programmer to understand the CPU operation in detail and the precise manner in which instruction bytes are packed into memory.

(b) *Assembly language*, i.e., write the program using mnemonics for the instruction opcode (e.g., MOV, OUT, etc.) and labels for addresses (e.g., START, LOOP). Although one instruction in assembly language converts into one machine code instruction, the hard work of generating opcodes and addresses in hex. is avoided.

(c) *High level language*, i.e., write the program using statements which are similar to spoken language. One such statement is converted into several machine code instructions before the program is run. The advantage of this technique is that long and complex programs can be written simply and quickly; also they can be transferred to other computers which possess the same language facility (e.g., BASIC, FORTRAN, PASCAL). However, high level language programs tend to be inefficient (fill large memory areas) and possess slow execution times. Also, fast and detailed input/output bit transfers are difficult to perform. Examples of BASIC statements are:

120 TOM = (CHARLIE + 100)*HARRY

i.e., a detailed arithmetic expression which converts into many machine code instructions—the statement number is 120.

1040 PRINT 'BUS TIMETABLE FOR SUNDAYS'

i.e., causes a message to be sent to a VDU or printer.

Although most programs for office and business microcomputer applications are written in a high level language, they are beyond the scope of this book. We are more concerned with the development of programs which can be entered and tested on training microcomputers in order to perform straightforward input/output tasks, e.g., washing machine controller, traffic light sequencer, digital clock, stepper motor drive.

The easiest way to develop programming ability is to enter programs into a training microcomputer and learn programming skills and debugging techniques by practical experience. It is assumed that the reader has access to one of the following types of computer trainers. Figure 7.1 shows the main components on a single-board training microcomputer.

The monitor program enables the programmer to enter his program via the keyboard, and to run and debug his program. Additionally, the contents of registers and memory locations can be displayed.

A typical entry and debugging procedure which is used through the monitor program is:

(a) Select the start address in memory (RAM) of the first instruction.

(b) Enter the program in machine code (or assembly language if available).

(c) Select the start address of program, i.e., set the program counter to first instruction in program.

(d) Execute the test program.

(e) Debug using:
   (1) execute to a breakpoint (i.e., stop at a selected address within the program);
   (2) single shot (i.e., obey one instruction at a time);
   (3) examine contents of registers and memory locations

A training board of this type can cost from £50 to £500. Typical examples are:

(a) Hewlett Packard HP5036A—based on the Intel 8085A;

(b) Multitech Micro-professor—based on the

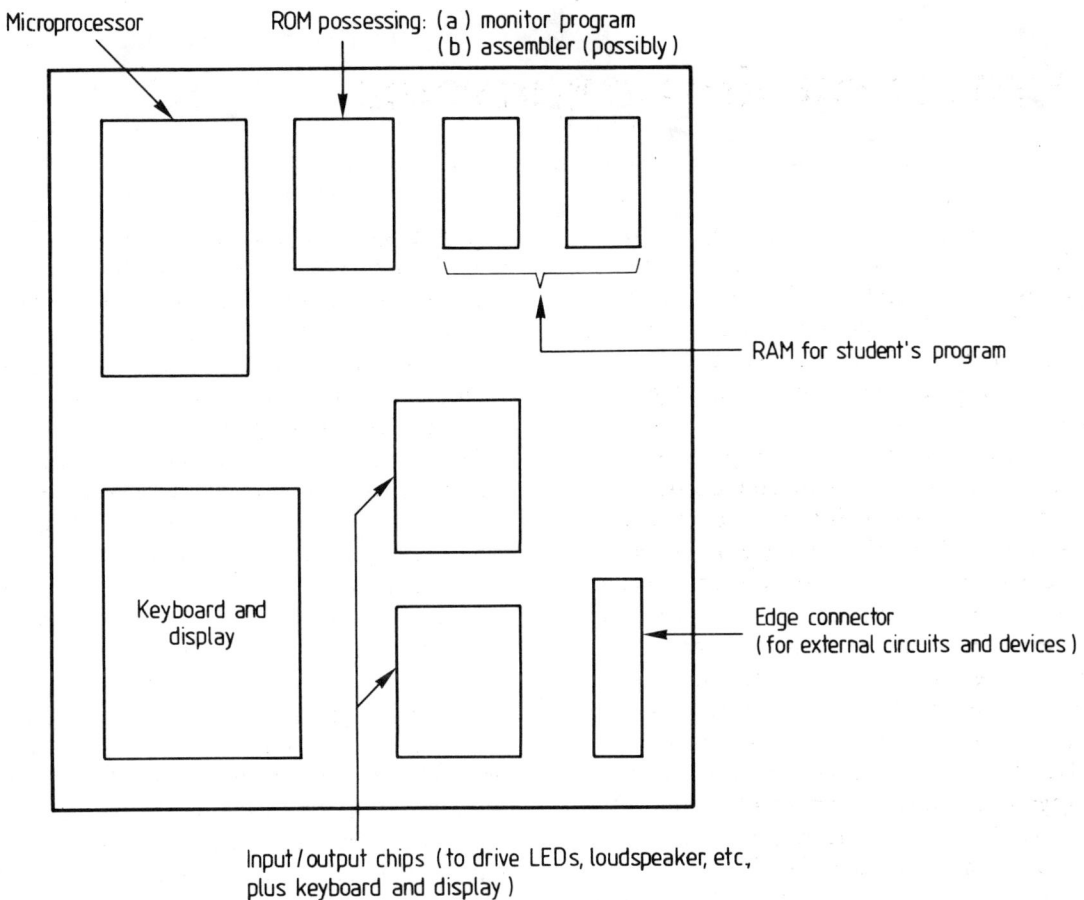

Figure 7.1 Typical single-board training microcomputer

Zilog Z80A;

(c) Rockwell AIM 65—based on the MOS Technology 6500;

(d) Texas Instruments University Board—based on the TI 9980A

The reader may be fortunate enough to have access to a full development system, which includes VDU, floppy disk, and printer. A typical system is shown in Fig. 7.2.

In this case the programmer has the following attractive features at his disposal:

(a) Floppy disk to give an assembler, an editor (to enter and alter his program), and a debugging program. The latter provides the debugging features of a monitor program, but uses the VDU for display purposes. Also, the programmer can store his program on disk; this avoids the necessity of reloading the program into RAM manually each time he wishes to test it.

(b) Printer to print out a listing of his program in assembly language and machine code with added comments.

(c) VDU and keyboard, which offer a more flexible and reliable interface than the small keyboard and segment digital display of the single-board microcomputer.

An **EPROM** programming facility is often available with such a system, so that a fully developed program can be transferred to a prototype board via a 2708 or 2716 **EPROM**.

The drawback with a system of this type is obviously its price, which can range from £1000 to £5000. Examples are:

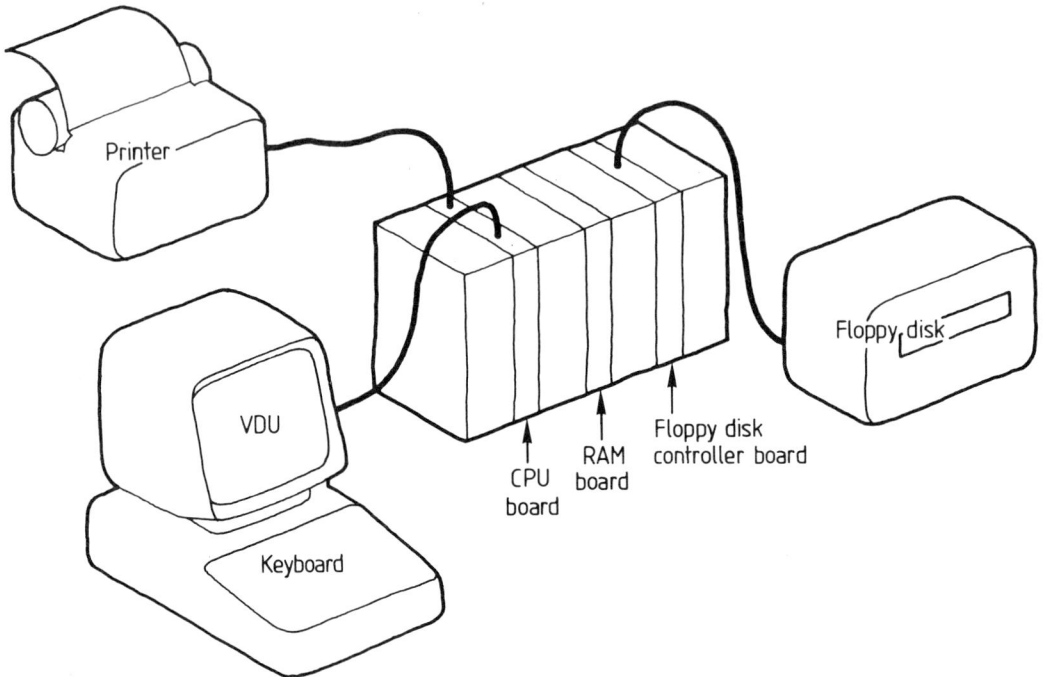

Figure 7.2 Program development system

(a) Intel Intellec MDS;
(b) Hewlett Packard Development System;
(c) Comcen S-100 Development System

Examples

1. Demonstrate the use of 'pseudo-instructions' in an assembly language program.

Answer:

```
            ORG 1000H
            TABLE EQU 3000H
START : MVI    A,0  ⎤
            |          ⎥
            |          ⎬ Program
            |          ⎥
            JMP START ⎦
            ORG TABLE
            DB 18,19,1A,1B
            END
```

The ORG, EQU, DB, and END commands, which are underlined above, are non-executable commands. This means that the assembler will not create machine code instructions for these commands. They are simply instructions to tell the assembler the following:

(a) ORG 1000H—commence assembly at memory location 1000.
(b) TABLE EQU 3000H—the EQU mnemonic stands for 'equate', and this command gives the value 3000 to the label TABLE; thus the command ORG TABLE transfers assembler control to memory location 3000.
(c) DB 18,19,1A,1B—DB stands for 'data byte', and this command places data bytes 18, 19, 1A, and 1B in memory locations 3000, 3001, 3002, and 3003.
(d) END—this tells the assembler that the program is complete; the assembler will then return to the monitor program (in the case of a small microcomputer trainer) or the operating system, i.e., master program (in the case of a disk system).

2. Write program sections which generate:
    (a) short delay (up to several milliseconds);
    (b) medium delay (up to nearly 1 second);
    (c) long delay (up to 3 minutes).

Answer: (a) Short delay:

```
        MVI  C,255      Set delay count
→ LOOP : DCR  C         Decrement delay count
│                       (four clock pulses)
└─────── JNZ  LOOP      Repeat 255 times
                        (ten or seven clock
                        pulses)
```

The DCR instruction takes four CPU clock periods (or 'machine cycles'—see Sec. 1.2, Example 7). The JNZ instruction takes 10 clock periods if the jump is performed, or seven clock periods if it is not. Thus a 2 MHz clock gives a loop delay time of:

$$254 \times (4+10) \times 0.5 \ \mu s \quad + \quad (4+7) \times 0.5 \ \mu s$$

First 254 passes through loop Last pass through loop

$$= 1783.5 \ \mu s = \text{approx. } 1.8 \ ms$$

This is the maximum delay which this loop can generate. If it is used in a subroutine as follows:

```
  SUB : MVI  C,255       Seven clock pulses
→ LOOP : DCR  C
│                        1783.5 μs delay
└─────── JNZ LOOP
        RET              10 clock pulses
```

then the total delay is $1783.5 + (7+10) \times 0.5 \ \mu s = 1792 \ \mu s$. A shorter delay can be achieved by calculating a smaller value for the loop count in register C.

(b) Medium delay:

An eight-bit count in register C can be replaced by a 16-bit count in the register pair B and C to produce a much longer delay for the Intel 8085. At first sight the following program would appear to provide a delay which is $2^8 = 256$ times longer than the delay in (a):

```
        LXI  B,FFFFH    Set delay count of
                        65 535 in register
                        pair BC
→ LOOP : DCX  B         Decrement delay
│                       count
└─────── JNZ  LOOP      Repeat 65 535 times
```

Unfortunately the DCX instruction does not set the zero flag in the status register, so the program will not run successfully. The following modified program is necessary:

```
        LXI  B,FFFFH    Set delay count of
                        65 535
→ LOOP : DCX  B         Decrement delay
│                       count (six clock
│                       pulses)
│       MOV A,B         Examine for both
│       ORA  C          B and C equal to
│                       zero (four clock
│                       pulses for each)
└─────── JNZ  LOOP      Repeat 65 535 times
                        (ten or seven clock
                        pulses)
```

Therefore, the loop delay time is:

$$65\,535 \times (6+4+4+10) \times 0.5 \ \mu s +$$
$$(6+4+4+7) \times 0.5 \ \mu s = 0.786 \ s$$

(c) Long delay:

If a delay of more than 0.786 s is required, then a nested loop arrangement offers the best solution:

```
          MVI  D,255       Outer loop count of 255
→ OUTER : LXI  B,FFFFH     Inner loop count of 65 535
│ → INNER : DCX  B
│ │       MOV  A,B         0.786 s delay in inner loop
│ │       ORA  C
│ └─────── JNZ  INNER
│         DCR  D
└───────── JNZ  OUTER      Repeat outer loop 255 times
```

Therefore, the total delay is approximately:

$$255 \times 0.786 \ s = 200 \ s$$

Delay routines of these types are required in a large range of applications:

(1) delays between keyboard scans;
(2) to generate pulses to a loudspeaker or stepper motor;
(3) delays between outputs to a traffic light LED sequence;
(4) delays in a washing machine controller or industrial sequence controller;
     etc.

3. Write a program which outputs pulses to a loudspeaker in order to generate a tone. (Note that a very similar program is required to drive a stepper motor.)

Answer: Assume the following hardware configuration:

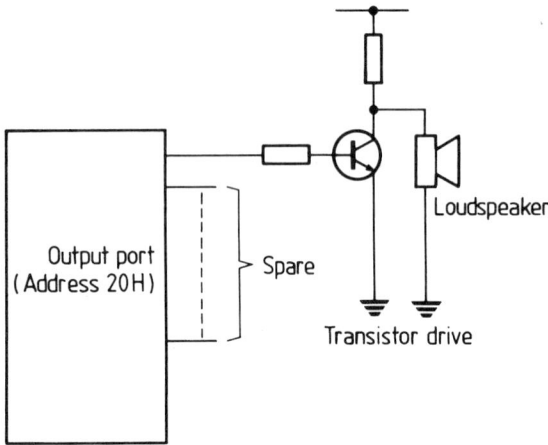

Algorithm:

Output a 1 (+5 V) to loudspeaker
Delay
Output a 0 (0 V) to loudspeaker
Delay
Repeat

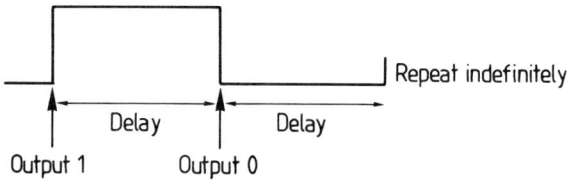

If the square wave is repeated, the loudspeaker diaphragm will vibrate continuously and a tone will be generated. The frequency of the note increases as the delay decreases.

Program:

```
TONE : MVI   A,1       Bit pattern of 0000 0001
       OUT   20H       Output to loudspeaker
       CALL  DELAY     Delay
       MVI   A,0       Bit pattern of 0000 0000
       OUT   20H       Output to loudspeaker
       CALL  DELAY     Delay
       JMP   TONE      Repeat
```

Subroutine:

```
DELAY : MVI   B,40  ⎫  Delay count of 40
LOOP  : DCR   B     ⎬  Loop 40 times
        JNZ   LOOP  ⎭
        RET           Return to main program
```

4. Write a program which plays a tune on a loudspeaker.

Answer: Assume the following data table:

Memory address

1000	Note 1 frequency (delay count)
1001	Note 1 length (number of square waves)
1002	Note 2 frequency
1003	Note 2 length
	etc.
	(total of eight notes)

Program:

```
  TUNE : LXI   H,1000H    Start address of data table
         MVI   E,8        Number of notes
  NOTE : MOV   B,M        Note frequency
         INX   H          Increment data table pointer
         MOV   D,M        Note length
         INX   H          Increment data table pointer
  PULSE: MVI   A,1
         OUT   20H
         MOV   C,B
         CALL  DELAY
         MVI   A,0
         OUT   20H
         MOV   C,B
         CALL  DELAY
         DCR   D
         JNZ   PULSE
         DCR   E
         JNZ   NOTE
         JMP   TUNE
```

One square wave (frequency set by delay in B)

One note (several square waves—number in D)

One tune (several notes—number in E)

Subroutine:

```
┌─►DELAY : DCR   C          ⎫
│              JNZ   DELAY   ⎬  Delay on C
└──────────── RET           ⎭
```

Notice the parameter passing when the subroutine is called—delay count is placed in register C.

5. Write a traffic light sequence program.
Answer: Assume the following hardware configuration:

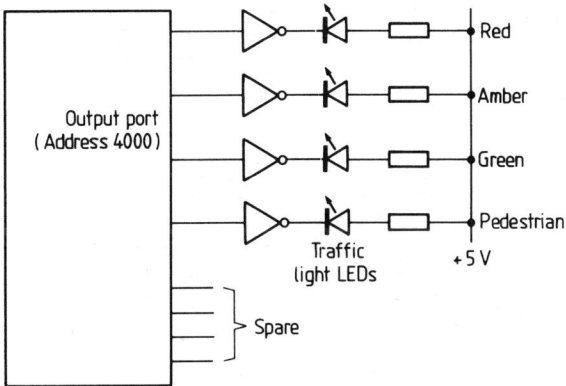

In this case it is assumed that input/output is memory mapped, which means:
(a) It is connected as a memory device.
(b) It fits into the memory map.
(c) Memory transfer instructions must be used in place of input/output instructions, i.e., STA in place of OUT.

The LED illumination sequence should be:
(1) Red
(2) Red + pedestrian
(3) Red
(4) Red + amber
(5) Green
(6) Amber
            Repeat

Assume that the same delay of approximately 10 seconds is used for each stage in the sequence and that the following data table is established:

Memory address

Address	Value	Description
2000	0000 0001	Red
2001	0000 1001	Red + pedestrian
2002	0000 0001	Red
2003	0000 0011	Red + amber
2004	0000 0100	Green
2005	0000 0010	Amber

Program:

```
┌─►START : LXI   H,2000H   Start address of data table
│          MVI   B,6       Number of stages in sequence
│ ┌─►LOOP : MOV  A,M        LED pattern
│ │        INX   H         Increment data table pointer
│ │        STA   4000H     Output bit pattern to LEDs
│ │        CALL  DELAY     Delay
│ │        DCR   B
│ └─────── JNZ   LOOP      Repeat six times
└───────── JMP   START
```

Subroutine:

```
  DELAY : MVI   C,13      Outer loop count of 13
┌─►OUTER : LXI   D,FFFFH   Inner loop count of 65 535 (in DE)
│┌─►INNER : DCX  D
││        MOV   A,D                0.786 s delay in inner loop
││        ORA   E
│└─────── JNZ   INNER
│         DCR   C
└──────── JNZ   OUTER     Repeat outer loop 13 times
          RET
```

The total delay is: 13×0.786 s = approx. 10 seconds.
    Notice that different registers are used in the subroutine compared with Example 2(c). This is necessary because the main program uses register B as a loop count.

6. Write a program which scans a keyboard and generates a note on a loudspeaker whenever a particular key is pressed. (Note: this is the 'skeleton' of an electronic organ program.)
Answer: Assume the following hardware configuration:

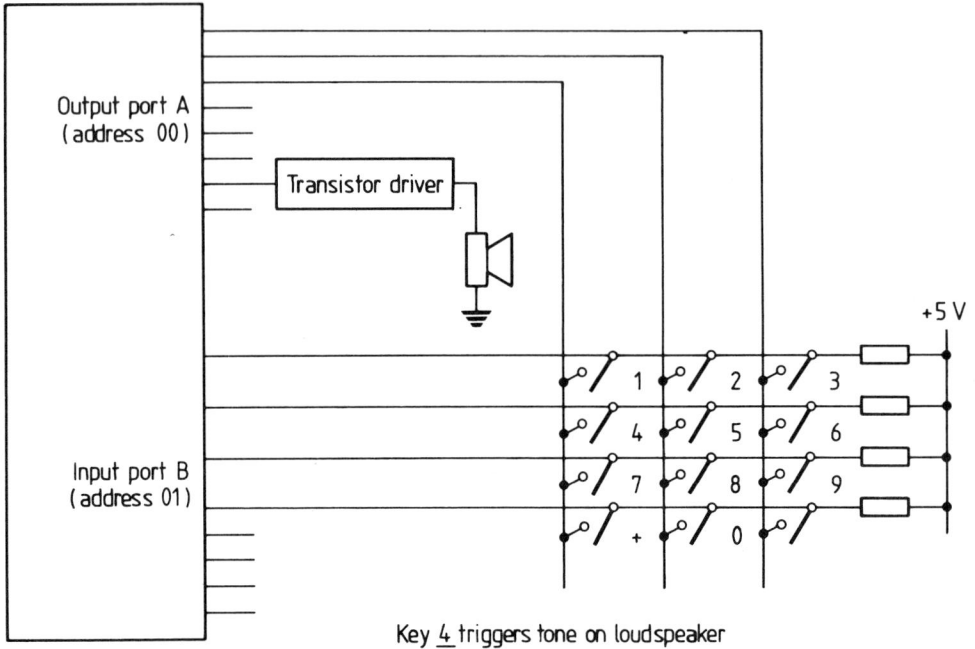

Key <u>4</u> triggers tone on loudspeaker

Flow chart:

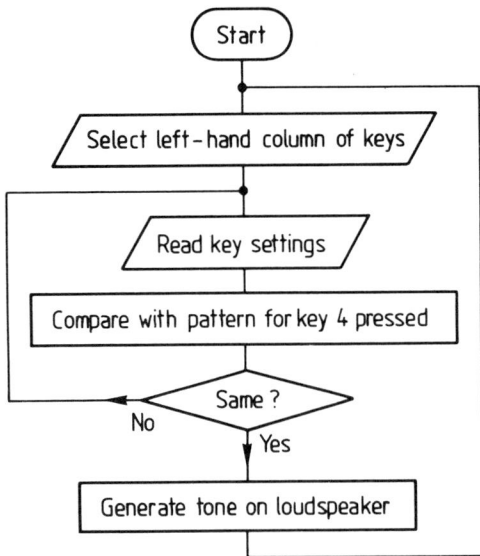

Program:

START:MVI	A,FBH	Bit pattern 1111 1011
OUT	00H	Set left-hand column to 0 V
SCAN:IN	01H	Read key settings
ANI	0FH	Mask out unused top four bits
CPI	0DH	Is key setting 1101?
JNZ	SCAN	Jump if not
CALL	NOTE	Generate note
JMP	START	Repeat

Subroutine:

NOTE:MVI	A,40H	Bit pattern 0100 0000
OUT	00H	Output 1 to loudspeaker
CALL	DELAY	Delay
MVI	A,00H	Bit pattern 0000 0000
OUT	00H	Output 0 to loudspeaker
CALL	DELAY	Delay
RET		

Nested subroutine:

DELAY:MVI	B,50	Delay loop count
LOOP:DCR	B	} Loop 50 times
JNZ	LOOP	
RET		

7. Write a program which uses an interval timer to generate a digital clock. A main program should update a segment display with the time of day, and an interrupt routine, which is activated by the interval timer, should update the time counts in memory.

Answer: Assume the following hardware configuration:

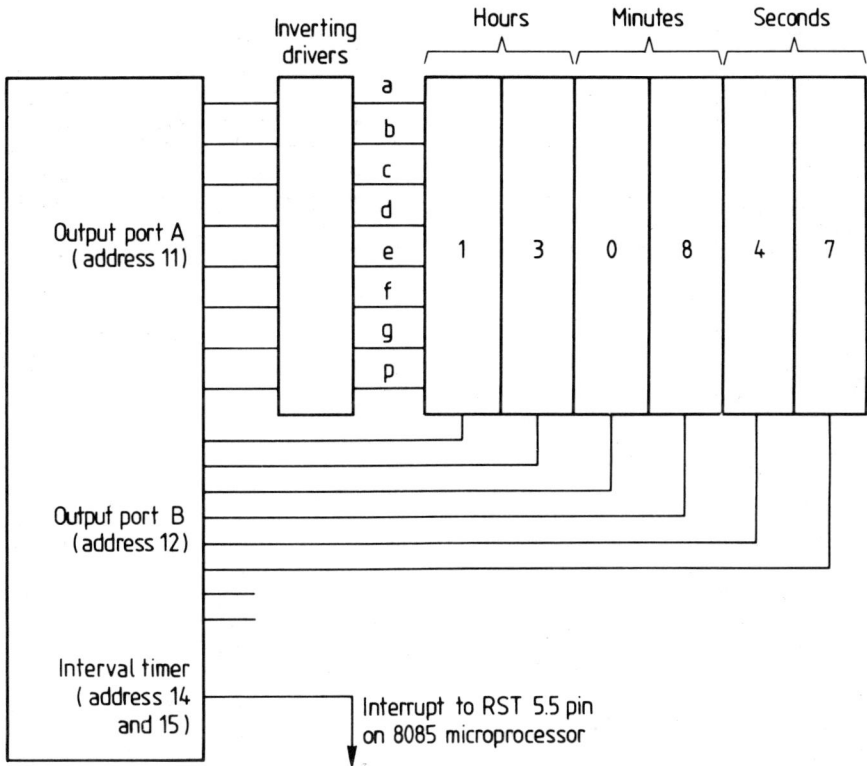

The following memory map, which includes two data tables, is required:

Memory address

Memory address	Contents		
0020	Jump to 1100		Interrupt vector for RST 5.5
1000	Main program (update display)		
1100	Interrupt routine (increment time counts)		
1200	0.001 second count		Data table 1 (time counts)
1201	0.1 second count		
1202	1 second count		
1203	10 second count		
1204	1 minute count		
1205	10 minute count		
1206	1 hour count		
1207	10 hour count		
1300	C0	0	Data table 2 (segment patterns for numbers 0 to 9, using inverse logic)
1301	F9	1	
1302	A4	2	
1303	B0	3	
1304	99	4	
1305	92	5	
1306	82	6	
1307	F8	7	
1308	80	8	
1309	90	9	
	↑ Expanding		
1400	Stack		

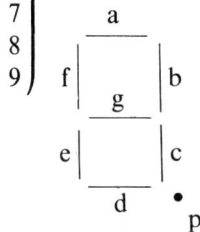

```
   a
 f|  |b
   g
 e|  |c
   d  •p
```

Main program:

```
              LXI   SP,1400H   Set stack pointer
              MVI   A,8
              LXI   H,1200H
CLEAR    : MVI   M,0      ⎫
              INX   H        ⎬ Zero all counts
              DCR   A        ⎭
              JNZ   CLEAR
              MVI   A,EOH    ⎫ Output low order half of
              OUT   14H      ⎭ count for 1 ms
              MVI   A,87H    ⎫ Output high order half
              OUT   15H      ⎭ of count for 1 ms
              MVI   A,C3H    ⎫ Output control bits to
              OUT   10H      ⎭ activate timer
              MVI   A,8      ⎫ Release interrupt mask
              SIM            ⎭ in CPU
              EI             Enable interrupt system
```

```
DISPLAY  : LXI   H,1202H   Address of first count
              MVI   B,6      Loop count for six displays
              MVI   C,20H    First (right-hand) display
                            — 0010 0000
LOOP     : LXI   D,1300H   Segment pattern data table
              MOV   A,M      Fetch count
              INX   H        Point to next count
              XCHG           Exchange D and E with H and L
              MOV   L,A      Set count in L of H and L
              MOV   A,M      Fetch segment pattern for count
              OUT   11H      Output segment pattern
              MOV   A,C      Display number
              OUT   12H      Output display number
              RRC            Select next display
              MOV   C,A      Reinstate display number in C
              XCHG           Exchange D and E with H and L
              DCR   B        ⎫ Display all six counts
              JNZ   LOOP     ⎭
              JMP   DISPLAY  Repeat display function
```

Interrupt routine:

```
              PUSH  PSW
              PUSH  H
              LXI   H,1200H
              INR   M        Increment 0.001 second count
              MVI   A,100    ⎫ Return unless hundredth
              CMP   M        ⎬ interrupt
              JNZ   RETURN   ⎭
              MVI   M,0      Zero 0.001 second count
```

```
              INX   H
              INR   M          Increment 0.1 second
                               count
              MVI   A,10
              CMP   M        } Return unless 0.1 second
              JNZ   RETURN     count has reached 10
              MVI   M,0        Zero 0.1 second count
- - - - - - - - - - - - - - - - - - - - - - - - - - - -
              INX   H
              INR   M          Increment 1 second
                               count
              MVI   A,10
              CMP   M        } Return unless 1 second
              JNZ   RETURN     count has reached 10
              MVI   M,0        Zero 1 second count
- - - - - - - - - - - - - - - - - - - - - - - - - - - -
              INX   H
              INR   M          Increment 10 second
                               count
              MVI   A,6
              CMP   M        } Return unless 10 second
              JNZ   RETURN     count has reached 6
              MVI   M,0        Zero 10 second count
- - - - - - - - - - - - - - - - - - - - - - - - - - - -
              INX   H
              INR   M          Increment 1 minute
                               count
              MVI   A,10
              CMP   M        } Return unless 1 minute
              JNZ   RETURN     count has reached 10
              MVI   M,0        Zero 1 minute count
- - - - - - - - - - - - - - - - - - - - - - - - - - - -
              INX   H
              INR   M          Increment 10 minute
                               count
              MVI   A,6
              CMP   M        } Return unless 10 minute
              JNZ   RETURN     count has reached 6
              MVI   M,0        Zero 10 minute count
- - - - - - - - - - - - - - - - - - - - - - - - - - - -
              INX   H
              INR   M          Increment 1 hour count
              MVI   A,4        Continue if not 4 hours
              CMP   M          — looking for 24 hours
              JNZ   NOTFOUR
              INX   H
              JMP   MIDNIGHT   Jump to midnight test
NOTFOUR : MVI   A,10
              CMP   M        } Return unless 1 hour
              JNZ   RETURN     count has reached 10
              MVI   M,0        Zero 1 hour count
- - - - - - - - - - - - - - - - - - - - - - - - - - - -

                INX   H
                INR   M          Increment 10 hour count
MIDNIGHT : MVI   A,2
                CMP   M        } Return if less than 20
                JNZ   RETURN     hours
                DCX   H          Change to 1 hour count
                MVI   A,4
                CMP   M        } Return unless 24 hours
                JNZ   RETURN     — midnight
                MVI   M,0        Zero 1 hour count
                INX   H          Change back to 10 hour
                                 count
                MVI   M,0        Zero 10 hour count
- - - - - - - - - - - - - - - - - - - - - - - - - - - -
RETURN    : POP   H
                POP   PSW
                RET
```

Interrupt vector:

```
              JMP   1100H      Jump to interrupt
                               routine
```

Notice that the main program consists of two sections:

(a) Initialize the interval timer to perform interrupts and clear all counts in memory — these counts could be loaded with the precise time when the program is activated first.

(b) Continuous update of segment display with the time of day — every 1 ms this loop is interrupted so that the interrupt routine can update the time counts in memory.

Exercises

1. What is machine code?

2. Name three high level languages.

3. What is a pseudo-instruction in an assembler?

4. State two advantages of programming in assembly language compared with machine code.

5. Which program must be ROM-based in a small microcomputer trainer?

6. What is a program 'breakpoint'? What does 'single shot' mean?

7. What two software development utility programs would you expect to find on a floppy disk in a full development system?

8. Examine Example 2 and write a subroutine which generates a time delay of 1 second.

9. Write a program which drives a stepper motor (address 10) continuously. The pulse waveform should be:

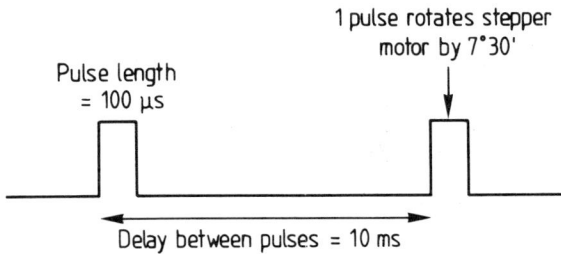

10. Write a traffic light sequencer program which:
    (a) uses different delays for each stage in the sequence;
    (b) generates a buzz on a loudspeaker during the pedestrian stage in the sequence

11. Write a program which generates a tune of precise frequencies. Note the frequencies are as follows:

$A = 450$ Hz, $B = 480$ Hz, $C = 540$ Hz, $D = 607$ Hz, $E = 675$ Hz, $F = 720$ Hz, $G = 810$ Hz
A (next octave) $= 900$ Hz, etc.

12. Write a program which generates a continuous tone on a loudspeaker, and an interrupt routine (driven by an interval timer) which flashes a LED for a short duration.

13. Write a stopwatch program which displays the duration between successive presses of a manual pushbutton. Use an interval timer interrupt to provide accurate timing.

14. Examine Example 7 and observe the repetitive use of a similar section of program coding for updating each count in the interrupt routine. Re-write the interrupt routine using a subroutine to perform this count update function.

15. Write an electronic musical keyboard program which scans a set of eight keys on a manual keyboard and generates a different tone on a loudspeaker when any of these keys is pressed.

Appendix

8085
SINGLE CHIP 8-BIT N-CHANNEL MICROPROCESSOR

- Single +5V Power Supply
- 100% Software Compatible with 8080A
- 1.3 µs Instruction Cycle
- On-Chip Clock Generator (with External Crystal or RC Network)
- On-Chip System Controller

- Four Vectored Interrupts (One is non-Maskable)
- Serial In/Serial Out Port
- Decimal, Binary and Double Precision Arithmetic
- Direct Addressing Capability to 64K Bytes of Memory

The Intel® 8085 is a new generation, complete 8 bit parallel central processing unit (CPU). Its instruction set is 100% software compatible with the 8080A microprocessor, and it is designed to improve the present 8080's performance by higher system speed. Its high level of system integration allows a minimum system of three IC's: 8085 (CPU), 8155 (RAM) and 8355/8755 (ROM/PROM).

The 8085 incorporates all of the features that the 8224 (clock generator) and 8228 (system controller) provided for the 8080, thereby offering a high level of system integration.

The 8085 uses a multiplexed Data Bus. The address is split between the 8 bit address bus and the 8 bit data bus. The on-chip address latches of 8155/8355/8755 memory products allows a direct interface with 8085.

8085 CPU FUNCTIONAL BLOCK DIAGRAM

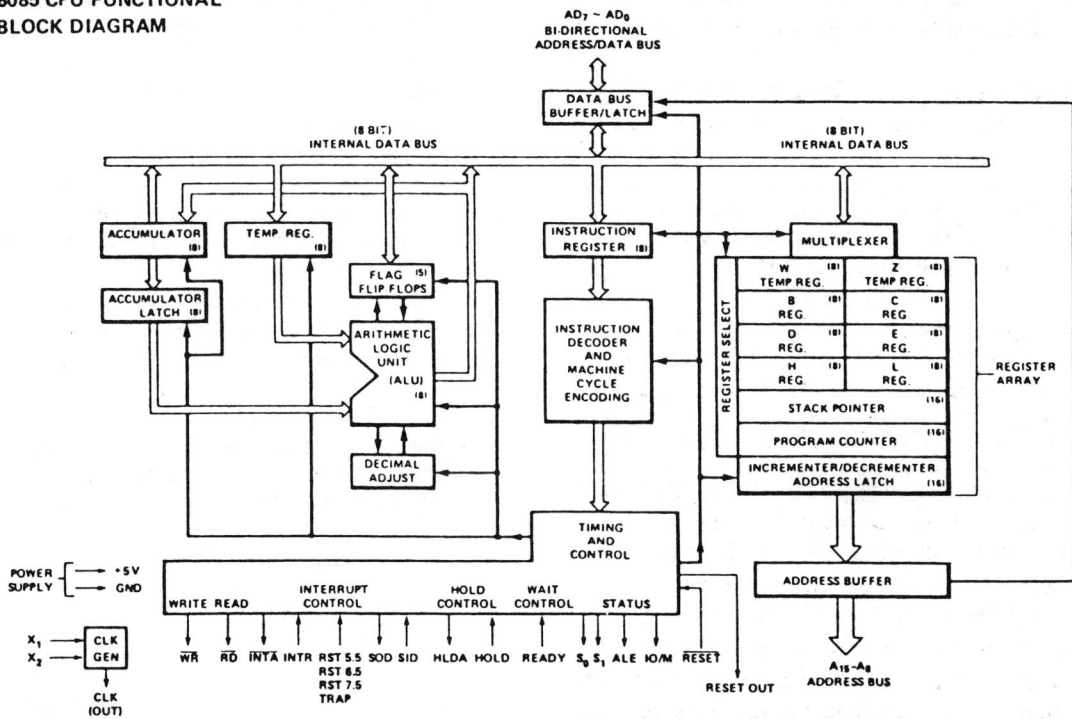

8085
INSTRUCTION SET*

A computer, no matter how sophisticated, can only do what it is "told" to do. One "tells" the computer what to do via a series of coded instructions referred to as a Program. The realm of the programmer is referred to as Software, in contrast to the Hardware that comprises the actual computer equipment. A computer's software refers to all of the programs that have been written for that computer.

When a computer is designed, the engineers provide the Central Processing Unit (CPU) with the ability to perform a particular set of operations. The CPU is designed such that a specific operation is performed when the CPU control logic decodes a particular instruction. Consequently, the operations that can be performed by a CPU define the computer's Instruction Set.

Each computer instruction allows the programmer to initiate the performance of a specific operation. All computers implement certain arithmetic operations in their instruction set, such as an instruction to add the contents of two registers. Often logical operations (e.g., OR the contents of two registers) and register operate instructions (e.g., increment a register) are included in the instruction set. A computer's instruction set will also have instructions that move data between registers, between a register and memory, and between a register and an I/O device. Most instruction sets also provide Conditional Instructions. A conditional instruction specifies an operation to be performed only if certain conditions have been met; for example, jump to a particular instruction if the result of the last operation was zero. Conditional instructions provide a program with a decision-making capability.

By logically organizing a sequence of instructions into a coherent program, the programmer can "tell" the computer to perform a very specific and useful function.

The computer, however, can only execute programs whose instructions are in a binary coded form (i.e., a series of 1's and 0's), that is called Machine Code. Because it would be extremely cumbersome to program in machine code, programming languages have been developed. There are programs available which convert the programming language instructions into machine code that can be interpreted by the processor.

One type of programming language is Assembly Language. A unique assembly language mnemonic is assigned to each of the computer's instructions. The programmer can write a program (called the Source Program) using these mnemonics and certain operands; the source program is then converted into machine instructions (called the Object Code). Each assembly language instruction is converted into one machine code instruction (1 or more bytes) by an Assembler program. Assembly languages are usually machine dependent (i.e., they are usually able to run on only one type of computer).

THE 8085 INSTRUCTION SET

The 8085 instruction set includes five different types of instructions:

- Data Transfer Group—move data between registers or between memory and registers

- Arithmetic Group — add, subtract, increment or decrement data in registers or in memory

- Logical Group — AND, OR, EXCLUSIVE-OR, compare, rotate or complement data in registers or in memory

- Branch Group — conditional and unconditional jump instructions, subroutine call instructions and return instructions

- Stack, I/O and Machine Control Group — includes I/O instructions, as well as instructions for maintaining the stack and internal control flags.

Instruction and Data Formats:

Memory for the 8085 is organized into 8-bit quantities, called Bytes. Each byte has a unique 16-bit binary address corresponding to its sequential position in memory.

---

*All mnemonics copyright © Intel Corporation 1976.

The 8085 can directly address up to 65,536 bytes of memory, which may consist of both read-only memory (ROM) elements and random-access memory (RAM) elements (read/write memory).

Data in the 8085 is stored in the form of 8-bit binary integers:

DATA WORD

D_7	D_6	D_5	D_4	D_3	D_2	D_1	D_0

MSB   LSB

When a register or data word contains a binary number, it is necessary to establish the order in which the bits of the number are written. In the Intel 8085, BIT 0 is referred to as the **Least Significant Bit (LSB)**, and BIT 7 (of an 8 bit number) is referred to as the **Most Significant Bit (MSB)**.

The 8085 program instructions may be one, two or three bytes in length. Multiple byte instructions must be stored in successive memory locations; the address of the first byte is always used as the address of the instructions. The exact instruction format will depend on the particular operation to be executed.

Single Byte Instructions

| D_7 | | | | | | | D_0 | Op Code |

Two-Byte Instructions

Byte One | D_7 | | | | | | | D_0 | Op Code

Byte Two | D_7 | | | | | | | D_0 | Data or Address

Three-Byte Instructions

Byte One | D_7 | | | | | | | D_0 | Op Code

Byte Two | D_7 | | | | | | | D_0 | Data

Byte Three | D_7 | | | | | | | D_0 | or Address

Addressing Modes:

Often the data that is to be operated on is stored in memory. When multi-byte numeric data is used, the data, like instructions, is stored in successive memory locations, with the least significant byte first, followed by increasingly significant bytes. The 8085 has four different modes for addressing data stored in memory or in registers:

- Direct — Bytes 2 and 3 of the instruction contain the exact memory address of the data item (the low-order bits of the address are in byte 2, the high-order bits in byte 3).
- Register — The instruction specifies the register or register-pair in which the data is located.
- Register Indirect — The instruction specifies a register-pair which contains the memory address where the data is located (the high-order bits of the address are in the first register of the pair, the low-order bits in the second).
- Immediate — The instruction contains the data itself. This is either an 8-bit quantity or a 16-bit quantity (least significant byte first, most significant byte second).

Unless directed by an interrupt or branch instruction, the execution of instructions proceeds through consecutively increasing memory locations. A branch instruction can specify the address of the next instruction to be executed in one of two ways:

- Direct — The branch instruction contains the address of the next instruction to be executed. (Except for the 'RST' instruction, byte 2 contains the low-order address and byte 3 the high-order address.)
- Register indirect — The branch instruction indicates a register-pair which contains the address of the next instruction to be executed. (The high-order bits of the address are in the first register of the pair, the low-order bits in the second.)

The RST instruction is a special one-byte call instruction (usually used during interrupt sequences). RST includes a three-bit field; program control is transferred to the instruction whose address is eight times the contents of this three-bit field.

Condition Flags:

There are five condition flags associated with the execution of instructions on the 8085. They are Zero, Sign, Parity, Carry, and Auxiliary Carry, and are each represented by a 1-bit register in the CPU. A flag is "set" by forcing the bit to 1, "reset" by forcing the bit to 0.

Unless indicated otherwise, when an instruction affects a flag, it affects it in the following manner:

Zero: If the result of an instruction has the value 0, this flag is set; otherwise it is reset.

Sign: If the most significant bit of the result of the operation has the value 1, this flag is set; otherwise it is reset.

Parity: If the modulo 2 sum of the bits of the result of the operation is 0, (i.e., if the result has even parity), this flag is set; otherwise it is reset (i.e., if the result has odd parity).

Carry: If the instruction resulted in a carry (from addition), or a borrow (from subtraction or a comparison) out of the high-order bit, this flag is set; otherwise it is reset.

Auxiliary Carry: If the instruction caused a carry out of bit 3 and into bit 4 of the resulting value, the auxiliary carry is set; otherwise it is reset. This flag is affected by single precision additions, subtractions, increments, decrements, comparisons, and logical operations, but is principally used with additions and increments preceding a DAA (Decimal Adjust Accumulator) instruction.

Symbols and Abbreviations:

The following symbols and abbreviations are used in the subsequent description of the 8085 instructions:

SYMBOLS	MEANING
accumulator	Register A
addr	16-bit address quantity
data	8-bit data quantity
data 16	16-bit data quantity
byte 2	The second byte of the instruction
byte 3	The third byte of the instruction
port	8-bit address of an I/O device
r,r1,r2	One of the registers A,B,C,D,E,H,L
DDD,SSS	The bit pattern designating one of the registers A,B,C,D,E,H,L (DDD=destination, SSS= source):

DDD or SSS	REGISTER NAME
111	A
000	B
001	C
010	D
011	E
100	H
101	L

rp   One of the register pairs:

B represents the B,C pair with B as the high-order register and C as the low-order register;

D represents the D,E pair with D as the high-order register and E as the low-order register;

H represents the H,L pair with H as the high-order register and L as the low-order register;

SP represents the 16-bit stack pointer register.

RP   The bit pattern designating one of the register pairs B,D,H,SP:

RP	REGISTER PAIR
00	B-C
01	D-E
10	H-L
11	SP

rh	The first (high-order) register of a designated register pair.
rl	The second (low-order) register of a designated register pair.
PC	16-bit program counter register (PCH and PCL are used to refer to the high-order and low-order 8 bits respectively).
SP	16-bit stack pointer register (SPH and SPL are used to refer to the high-order and low-order 8 bits respectively).
r_m	Bit m of the register r (bits are number 7 through 0 from left to right).
Z,S,P,CY,AC	The condition flags:

           Zero,
           Sign,
           Parity,
           Carry,
           and Auxiliary Carry, respectively.

( )	The contents of the memory location or registers enclosed in the parentheses.
←	"Is transferred to"
∧	Logical AND
∀	Exclusive OR
∨	Inclusive OR
+	Addition
−	Two's complement subtraction
*	Multiplication
↔	"Is exchanged with"
‾	The one's complement (e.g., $(\overline{A})$)
n	The restart number 0 through 7
NNN	The binary representation 000 through 111 for restart number 0 through 7 respectively.

Description Format:

The following pages provide a detailed description of the instruction set of the 8085. Each instruction is described in the following manner:

1. The MCS 85™ macro assembler format, consisting of the instruction mnemonic and operand fields, is printed in **BOLDFACE** on the left side of the first line.

2. The name of the instruction is enclosed in parenthesis on the right side of the first line.

3. The next line(s) contain a symbolic description of the operation of the instruction.

4. This is followed by a narative description of the operation of the instruction.

5. The following line(s) contain the binary fields and patterns that comprise the machine instruction.

6. The last four lines contain incidental information, about the execution of the instruction. The number of machine cycles and states required to execute the instruction are listed first. If the instruction has two possible execution times, as in a Conditional Jump, both times will be listed, separated by a slash. Next, any significant data addressing modes (see Page 4-2) are listed. The last line lists any of the five Flags that are affected by the execution of the instruction.

Data Transfer Group:

This group of instructions transfers data to and from registers and memory. Condition flags are not affected by any instruction in this group.

MOV r1, r2 (Move Register)

(r1) ◄── (r2)

The content of register r2 is moved to register r1.

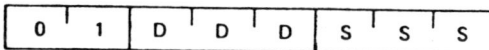

0	1	D	D	D	S	S	S

Cycles: 1
States: 4
Addressing: register
Flags: none

MOV r, M (Move from memory)

(r) ◄── ((H) (L))

The content of the memory location, whose address is in registers H and L, is moved to register r.

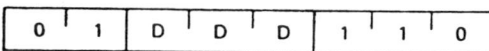

0	1	D	D	D	1	1	0

Cycles: 2
States: 7
Addressing: reg. indirect
Flags: none

MOV M, r (Move to memory)

((H) (L)) ◄── (r)

The content of register r is moved to the memory location whose address is in registers H and L.

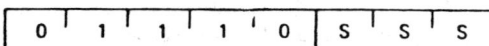

0	1	1	1	0	S	S	S

Cycles: 2
States: 7
Addressing: reg. indirect
Flags: none

MVI r, data (Move Immediate)

(r) ◄── (byte 2)

The content of byte 2 of the instruction is moved to register r.

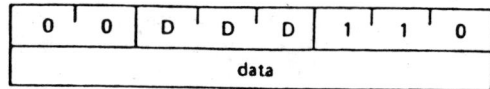

0	0	D	D	D	1	1	0
data							

Cycles: 2
States: 7
Addressing: immediate
Flags: none

MVI M, data (Move to memory immediate)

((H) (L)) ◄── (byte 2)

The content of byte 2 of the instruction is moved to the memory location whose address is in registers H and L.

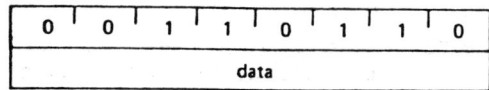

0	0	1	1	0	1	1	0
data							

Cycles: 3
States: 10
Addressing: immed./reg. indirect
Flags: none

LXI rp, data 16 (Load register pair immediate)

(rh) ◄── (byte 3),

(rl) ◄── (byte 2)

Byte 3 of the instruction is moved into the high-order register (rh) of the register pair rp. Byte 2 of the instruction is moved into the low-order register (rl) of the register pair rp.

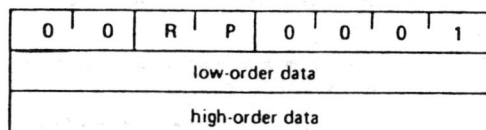

0	0	R	P	0	0	0	1
low-order data							
high-order data							

Cycles: 3
States: 10
Addressing: immediate
Flags: none

LDA addr   (Load Accumulator direct)

(A) ⟵ ((byte 3)(byte 2))

The content of the memory location, whose address is specified in byte 2 and byte 3 of the instruction, is moved to register A.

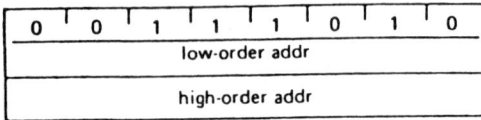

0	0	1	1	1	0	1	0
low-order addr							
high-order addr							

Cycles: 4
States: 13
Addressing: direct
Flags: none

STA addr   (Store Accumulator direct)

((byte 3)(byte 2)) ⟵ (A)

The content of the accumulator is moved to the memory location whose address is specified in byte 2 and byte 3 of the instruction.

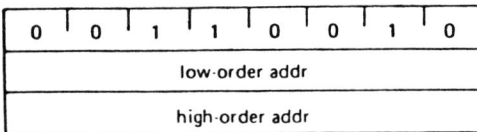

0	0	1	1	0	0	1	0
low-order addr							
high-order addr							

Cycles: 4
States: 13
Addressing: direct
Flags: none

LHLD addr   (Load H and L direct)

(L) ⟵ ((byte 3)(byte 2))

(H) ⟵ ((byte 3)(byte 2) + 1)

The content of the memory location, whose address is specified in byte 2 and byte 3 of the instruction, is moved to register L. The content of the memory location at the succeeding address is moved to register H.

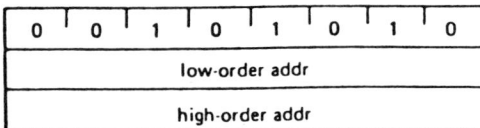

0	0	1	0	1	0	1	0
low-order addr							
high-order addr							

Cycles: 5
States: 16
Addressing: direct
Flags: none

SHLD addr   (Store H and L direct)

((byte 3)(byte 2)) ⟵ (L)

((byte 3)(byte 2) + 1) ⟵ (H)

The content of register L is moved to the memory location whose address is specified in byte 2 and byte 3. The content of register H is moved to the succeeding memory location.

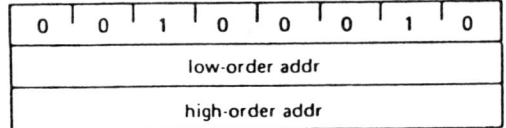

0	0	1	0	0	0	1	0
low-order addr							
high-order addr							

Cycles: 5
States: 16
Addressing: direct
Flags: none

LDAX rp   (Load accumulator indirect)

(A) ⟵ ((rp))

The content of the memory location, whose address is in the register pair rp, is moved to register A. Note: only register pairs rp=B (registers B and C) or rp=D (registers D and E) may be specified.

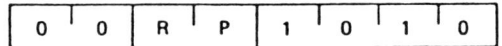

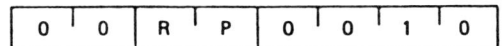

0	0	R	P	1	0	1	0

Cycles: 2
States: 7
Addressing: reg. indirect
Flags: none

STAX rp   (Store accumulator indirect)

((rp)) ⟵ (A)

The content of register A is moved to the memory location whose address is in the register pair rp. Note: only register pairs rp=B (registers B and C) or rp=D (registers D and E) may be specified.

0	0	R	P	0	0	1	0

Cycles: 2
States: 7
Addressing: reg. indirect
Flags: none

XCHG   (Exchange H and L with D and E)

(H) ⟷ (D)

(L) ⟷ (E)

The contents of registers H and L are exchanged with the contents of registers D and E.

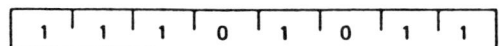

1	1	1	0	1	0	1	1

Cycles: 1
States: 4
Addressing: register
Flags: none

Arithmetic Group:

This group of instructions performs arithmetic operations on data in registers and memory.

Unless indicated otherwise, all instructions in this group affect the Zero, Sign, Parity, Carry, and Auxiliary Carry flags according to the standard rules.

All subtraction operations are performed via two's complement arithmetic and set the carry flag to one to indicate a borrow and clear it to indicate no borrow.

ADD r   (Add Register)
(A) ← (A) + (r)

The content of register r is added to the content of the accumulator. The result is placed in the accumulator.

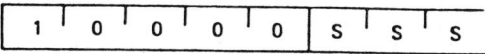

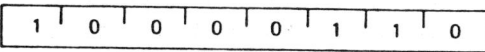

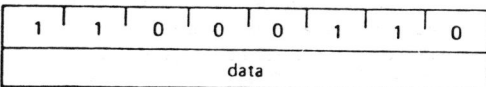

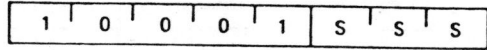

1	0	0	0	0	S	S	S

Cycles: 1
States: 4
Addressing: register
Flags: Z,S,P,CY,AC

ADD M   (Add memory)
(A) ← (A) + ((H) (L))

The content of the memory location whose address is contained in the H and L registers is added to the content of the accumulator. The result is placed in the accumulator.

1	0	0	0	0	1	1	0

Cycles: 2
States: 7
Addressing: reg. indirect
Flags: Z,S,P,CY,AC

ADI data   (Add immediate)
(A) ← (A) + (byte 2)

The content of the second byte of the instruction is added to the content of the accumulator. The result is placed in the accumulator.

1	1	0	0	0	1	1	0
data

Cycles: 2
States: 7
Addressing: immediate
Flags: Z,S,P,CY,AC

ADC r   (Add Register with carry)
(A) ← (A) + (r) + (CY)

The content of register r and the content of the carry bit are added to the content of the accumulator. The result is placed in the accumulator.

1	0	0	0	1	S	S	S

Cycles: 1
States: 4
Addressing: register
Flags: Z,S,P,CY,AC

ADC M   (Add memory with carry)
(A) ← (A) + ((H) (L)) + (CY)

The content of the memory location whose address is contained in the H and L registers and the content of the CY flag are added to the accumulator. The result is placed in the accumulator.

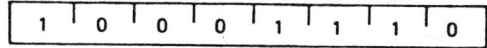

1	0	0	0	1	1	1	0

Cycles: 2
States: 7
Addressing: reg. indirect
Flags: Z,S,P,CY,AC

ACI data   (Add immediate with carry)
(A) ← (A) + (byte 2) + (CY)

The content of the second byte of the instruction and the content of the CY flag are added to the contents of the accumulator. The result is placed in the accumulator.

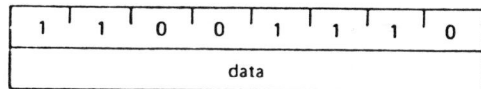

1	1	0	0	1	1	1	0
data

Cycles: 2
States: 7
Addressing: immediate
Flags: Z,S,P,CY,AC

SUB r   (Subtract Register)
(A) ← (A) − (r)

The content of register r is subtracted from the content of the accumulator. The result is placed in the accumulator.

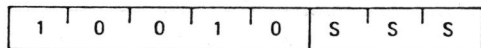

1	0	0	1	0	S	S	S

Cycles: 1
States: 4
Addressing: register
Flags: Z,S,P,CY,AC

SUB M   (Subtract memory)

(A) ←— (A) − ((H) (L))

The content of the memory location whose address is contained in the H and L registers is subtracted from the content of the accumulator. The result is placed in the accumulator.

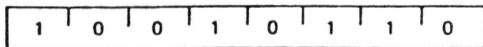

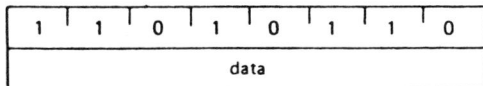

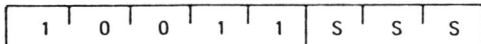

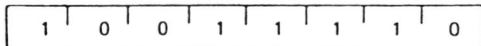

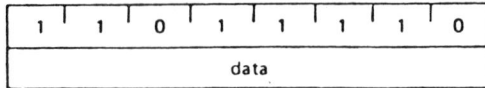

1	0	0	1	0	1	1	0

Cycles: 2
States: 7
Addressing: reg. indirect
Flags: Z,S,P,CY,AC

SUI data   (Subtract immediate)

(A) ←— (A) − (byte 2)

The content of the second byte of the instruction is subtracted from the content of the accumulator. The result is placed in the accumulator.

1	1	0	1	0	1	1	0
data							

Cycles: 2
States: 7
Addressing: immediate
Flags: Z,S,P,CY,AC

SBB r   (Subtract Register with borrow)

(A) ←— (A) − (r) − (CY)

The content of register r and the content of the CY flag are both subtracted from the accumulator. The result is placed in the accumulator.

1	0	0	1	1	S	S	S

Cycles: 1
States: 4
Addressing: register
Flags: Z,S,P,CY,AC

SBB M   (Subtract memory with borrow)

(A) ←— (A) − ((H) (L)) − (CY)

The content of the memory location whose address is contained in the H and L registers and the content of the CY flag are both subtracted from the accumulator. The result is placed in the accumulator.

1	0	0	1	1	1	1	0

Cycles: 2
States: 7
Addressing: reg. indirect
Flags: Z,S,P,CY,AC

SBI data   (Subtract immediate with borrow)

(A) ←— (A) − (byte 2) − (CY)

The contents of the second byte of the instruction and the contents of the CY flag are both subtracted from the accumulator. The result is placed in the accumulator.

1	1	0	1	1	1	1	0
data							

Cycles: 2
States: 7
Addressing: immediate
Flags: Z,S,P,CY,AC

INR r   (Increment Register)

(r) ←— (r) + 1

The content of register r is incremented by one. Note: All condition flags except CY are affected.

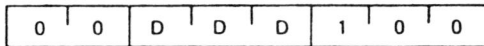

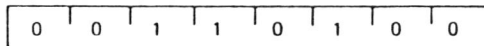

0	0	D	D	D	1	0	0

Cycles: 1
States: 4
Addressing: register
Flags: Z,S,P,AC

INR M   (Increment memory)

((H) (L)) ←— ((H) (L)) + 1

The content of the memory location whose address is contained in the H and L registers is incremented by one. Note: All condition flags except CY are affected.

0	0	1	1	0	1	0	0

Cycles: 3
States: 10
Addressing: reg. indirect
Flags: Z,S,P,AC

DCR r   (Decrement Register)

(r) ←— (r) − 1

The content of register r is decremented by one. Note: All condition flags except CY are affected.

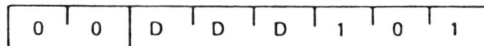

0	0	D	D	D	1	0	1

Cycles: 1
States: 4
Addressing: register
Flags: Z,S,P,AC

DCR M   (Decrement memory)

((H) (L)) ⟵ ((H) (L)) − 1

The content of the memory location whose address is contained in the H and L registers is decremented by one. Note: All condition flags **except CY** are affected.

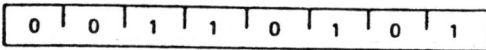

0	0	1	1	0	1	0	1

Cycles: 3
States: 10
Addressing: reg. indirect
Flags: Z,S,P,AC

INX rp   (Increment register pair)

(rh) (rl) ⟵ (rh) (rl) + 1

The content of the register pair rp is incremented by one. Note: **No condition flags are affected.**

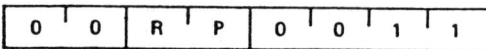

0	0	R	P	0	0	1	1

Cycles: 1
States: 6
Addressing: register
Flags: none

DCX rp   (Decrement register pair)

(rh) (rl) ⟵ (rh) (rl) − 1

The content of the register pair rp is decremented by one. Note: **No condition flags are affected.**

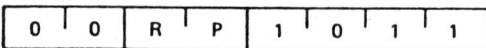

0	0	R	P	1	0	1	1

Cycles: 1
States: 6
Addressing: register
Flags: none

DAD rp   (Add register pair to H and L)

(H) (L) ⟵ (H) (L) + (rh) (rl)

The content of the register pair rp is added to the content of the register pair H and L. The result is placed in the register pair H and L. Note: Only the **CY flag is affected.** It is set if there is a carry out of the double precision add; otherwise it is reset.

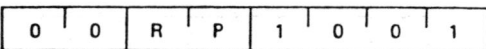

0	0	R	P	1	0	0	1

Cycles: 3
States: 10
Addressing: register
Flags: CY

DAA   (Decimal Adjust Accumulator)

The eight-bit number in the accumulator is adjusted to form two four-bit Binary-Coded-Decimal digits by the following process:

1.   If the value of the least significant 4 bits of the accumulator is greater than 9 or if the AC flag is set, 6 is added to the accumulator.

2.   If the value of the most significant 4 bits of the accumulator is now greater than 9, or if the CY flag is set, 6 is added to the most significant 4 bits of the accumulator.

NOTE: All flags are affected.

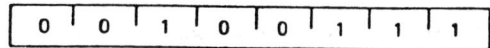

0	0	1	0	0	1	1	1

Cycles: 1
States: 4
Flags: Z,S,P,CY,AC

Logical Group:

This group of instructions performs logical (Boolean) operations on data in registers and memory and on condition flags.

Unless indicated otherwise, all instructions in this group affect the Zero, Sign, Parity, Auxiliary Carry, and Carry flags according to the standard rules.

ANA r   (AND Register)

(A) ⟵ (A) ∧ (r)

The content of register r is logically anded with the content of the accumulator. The result is placed in the accumulator. **The CY flag is cleared and AC is set.**

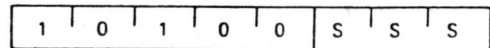

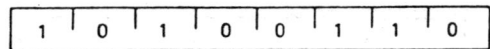

1	0	1	0	0	S	S	S

Cycles: 1
States: 4
Addressing: register
Flags: Z,S,P,CY,AC

ANA M   (AND memory)

(A) ⟵ (A) ∧ ((H) (L))

The contents of the memory location whose address is contained in the H and L registers is logically anded with the content of the accumulator. The result is placed in the accumulator. **The CY flag is cleared and AC is set.**

1	0	1	0	0	1	1	0

Cycles: 2
States: 7
Addressing: reg. indirect
Flags: Z,S,P,CY,AC

ANI data   (AND immediate)

(A) ←— (A) ∧ (byte 2)

The content of the second byte of the instruction is logically anded with the contents of the accumulator. The result is placed in the accumulator. **The CY flag is cleared and AC is set.**

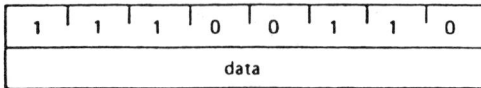

1	1	1	0	0	1	1	0
data							

Cycles: 2
States: 7
Addressing: immediate
Flags: Z,S,P,CY,AC

XRA r   (Exclusive OR Register)

(A) ←— (A) ∀ (r)

The content of register r is exclusive-or'd with the content of the accumulator. The result is placed in the accumulator. **The CY and AC flags are cleared.**

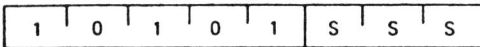

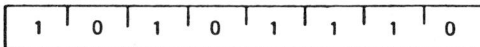

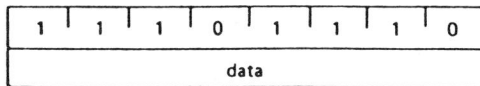

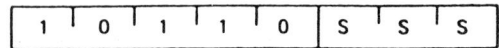

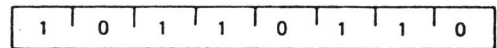

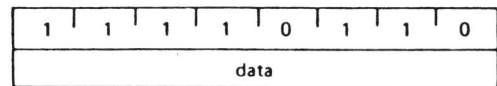

1	0	1	0	1	S	S	S

Cycles: 1
States: 4
Addressing: register
Flags: Z,S,P,CY,AC

XRA M   (Exclusive OR Memory)

(A) ←— (A) ∀ ((H) (L))

The content of the memory location whose address is contained in the H and L registers is exclusive-OR'd with the content of the accumulator. The result is placed in the accumulator. **The CY and AC flags are cleared.**

1	0	1	0	1	1	1	0

Cycles: 2
States: 7
Addressing: reg. indirect
Flags: Z,S,P,CY,AC

XRI data   (Exclusive OR immediate)

(A) ←— (A) ∀ (byte 2)

The content of the second byte of the instruction is exclusive-OR'd with the content of the accumulator. The result is placed in the accumulator. **The CY and AC flags are cleared.**

1	1	1	0	1	1	1	0
data							

Cycles: 2
States: 7
Addressing: immediate
Flags: Z,S,P,CY,AC

ORA r   (OR Register)

(A) ←— (A) V (r)

The content of register r is inclusive-OR'd with the content of the accumulator. The result is placed in the accumulator. **The CY and AC flags are cleared.**

1	0	1	1	0	S	S	S

Cycles: 1
States: 4
Addressing: register
Flags: Z,S,P,CY,AC

ORA M   (OR memory)

(A) ←— (A) V ((H) (L))

The content of the memory location whose address is contained in the H and L registers is inclusive-OR'd with the content of the accumulator. The result is placed in the accumulator. **The CY and AC flags are cleared.**

1	0	1	1	0	1	1	0

Cycles: 2
States: 7
Addressing: reg. indirect
Flags: Z,S,P,CY,AC

ORI data   (OR Immediate)

(A) ←— (A) V (byte 2)

The content of the second byte of the instruction is inclusive-OR'd with the content of the accumulator. The result is placed in the accumulator. **The CY and AC flags are cleared.**

1	1	1	1	0	1	1	0
data							

Cycles: 2
States: 7
Addressing: immediate
Flags: Z,S,P,CY,AC

CMP r   (Compare Register)

(A) − (r)

The content of register r is subtracted from the accumulator. The accumulator remains unchanged. The condition flags are set as a result of the subtraction. The Z flag is set to 1 if (A) = (r). The CY flag is set to 1 if (A) < (r).

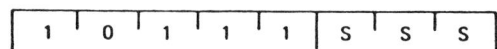

1	0	1	1	1	S	S	S

Cycles: 1
States: 4
Addressing: register
Flags: Z,S,P,CY,AC

CMP M (Compare memory)

(A) − ((H) (L))

The content of the memory location whose address is contained in the H and L registers is subtracted from the accumulator. The accumulator remains unchanged. The condition flags are set as a result of the subtraction. The Z flag is set to 1 if (A) = ((H) (L)). The CY flag is set to 1 if (A) < ((H) (L)).

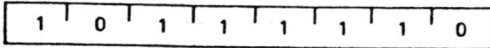

1	0	1	1	1	1	1	0

```
      Cycles:    2
      States:    7
  Addressing:    reg. indirect.
       Flags:    Z,S,P,CY,AC
```

CPI data (Compare immediate)

(A) − (byte 2)

The content of the second byte of the instruction is subtracted from the accumulator. The condition flags are set by the result of the subtraction. The Z flag is set to 1 if (A) = (byte 2). The CY flag is set to 1 if (A) < (byte 2).

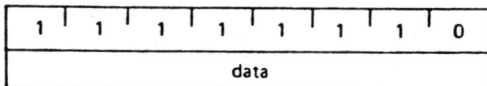

1	1	1	1	1	1	1	0
data							

```
      Cycles:    2
      States:    7
  Addressing:    immediate
       Flags:    Z,S,P,CY,AC
```

RLC (Rotate left)

$(A_{n+1}) \leftarrow (A_n) ; (A_0) \leftarrow (A_7)$
$(CY) \leftarrow (A_7)$

The content of the accumulator is rotated left one position. The low order bit and the CY flag are both set to the value shifted out of the high order bit position. Only the CY flag is affected.

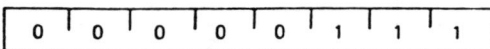

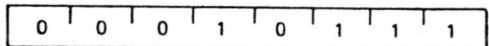

0	0	0	0	0	1	1	1

```
      Cycles:    1
      States:    4
       Flags:    CY
```

RRC (Rotate right)

$(A_n) \leftarrow (A_{n-1}) ; (A_7) \leftarrow (A_0)$
$(CY) \leftarrow (A_0)$

The content of the accumulator is rotated right one position. The high order bit and the CY flag are both set to the value shifted out of the low order bit position. Only the CY flag is affected.

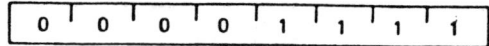

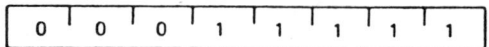

0	0	0	0	1	1	1	1

```
      Cycles:    1
      States:    4
       Flags:    CY
```

RAL (Rotate left through carry)

$(A_{n+1}) \leftarrow (A_n) ; (CY) \leftarrow (A_7)$
$(A_0) \leftarrow (CY)$

The content of the accumulator is rotated left one position through the CY flag. The low order bit is set equal to the CY flag and the CY flag is set to the value shifted out of the high order bit. Only the CY flag is affected.

0	0	0	1	0	1	1	1

```
      Cycles:    1
      States:    4
       Flags:    CY
```

RAR (Rotate right through carry)

$(A_n) \leftarrow (A_{n+1}) ; (CY) \leftarrow (A_0)$
$(A_7) \leftarrow (CY)$

The content of the accumulator is rotated right one position through the CY flag. The high order bit is set to the CY flag and the CY flag is set to the value shifted out of the low order bit. Only the CY flag is affected.

0	0	0	1	1	1	1	1

```
      Cycles:    1
      States:    4
       Flags:    CY
```

CMA (Complement accumulator)

$(A) \leftarrow (\overline{A})$

The contents of the accumulator are complemented (zero bits become 1, one bits become 0). No flags are affected.

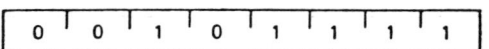

0	0	1	0	1	1	1	1

```
      Cycles:    1
      States:    4
       Flags:    none
```

CMC (Complement carry)

(CY) ← (CY̅)

The CY flag is complemented. No other flags are affected.

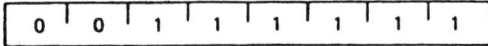

0	0	1	1	1	1	1	1

Cycles: 1
States: 4
Flags: CY

STC (Set carry)

(CY) ← 1

The CY flag is set to 1. No other flags are affected.

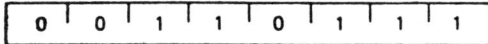

0	0	1	1	0	1	1	1

Cycles: 1
States: 4
Flags: CY

Branch Group:

This group of instructions alter normal sequential program flow.

Condition flags are not affected by any instruction in this group.

The two types of branch instructions are unconditional and conditional. Unconditional transfers simply perform the specified operation on register PC (the program counter). Conditional transfers examine the status of one of the four processor flags to determine if the specified branch is to be executed. The conditions that may be specified are as follows:

CONDITION		CCC
NZ	— not zero (Z = 0)	000
Z	— zero (Z = 1)	001
NC	— no carry (CY = 0)	010
C	— carry (CY = 1)	011
PO	— parity odd (P = 0)	100
PE	— parity even (P = 1)	101
P	— plus (S = 0)	110
M	— minus (S = 1)	111

JMP addr (Jump)

(PC) ← (byte 3) (byte 2)

Control is transferred to the instruction whose ad-dress is specified in byte 3 and byte 2 of the current instruction.

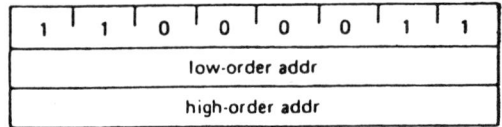

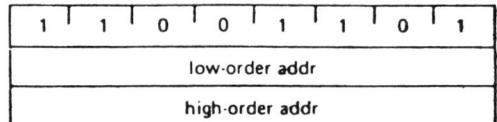

1	1	0	0	0	0	1	1
low-order addr							
high-order addr							

Cycles: 3
States: 10
Addressing: immediate
Flags: none

Jcondition addr (Conditional jump)

If (CCC),

(PC) ← (byte 3) (byte 2)

If the specified condition is true, control is transferred to the instruction whose address is specified in byte 3 and byte 2 of the current instruction; otherwise, control continues sequentially.

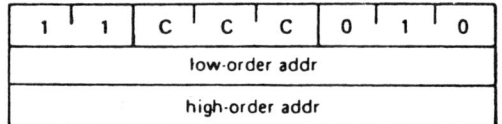

1	1	C	C	C	0	1	0
low-order addr							
high-order addr							

Cycles: 2/3
States: 7/10
Addressing: immediate
Flags: none

CALL addr (Call)

((SP) − 1) ← (PCH)
((SP) − 2) ← (PCL)
(SP) ← (SP) − 2
(PC) ← (byte 3) (byte 2)

The high-order eight bits of the next instruction address are moved to the memory location whose address is one less than the content of register SP. The low-order eight bits of the next instruction address are moved to the memory location whose address is two less than the content of register SP. The content of register SP is decremented by 2. Control is transferred to the instruction whose address is specified in byte 3 and byte 2 of the current instruction.

1	1	0	0	1	1	0	1
low-order addr							
high-order addr							

Cycles: 5
States: 18
Addressing: immediate/reg. indirect
Flags: none

Ccondition addr   (Condition call)

If (CCC),

((SP) − 1) ◄— (PCH)

((SP) − 2) ◄— (PCL)

(SP) ◄— (SP) − 2

(PC) ◄— (byte 3) (byte 2)

If the specified condition is true, the actions specified in the CALL instruction (see above) are performed; otherwise, control continues sequentially.

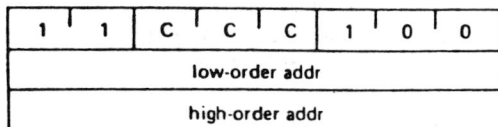

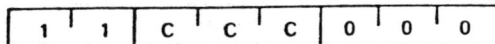

1	1	C	C	C	1	0	0
low-order addr							
high-order addr							

Cycles: 2/5

States: 9/18

Addressing: immediate/reg. indirect

Flags: none

RET   (Return)

(PCL) ◄— ((SP));

(PCH) ◄— ((SP) + 1);

(SP) ◄— (SP) + 2;

The content of the memory location whose address is specified in register SP is moved to the low-order eight bits of register PC. The content of the memory location whose address is one more than the content of register SP is moved to the high-order eight bits of register PC. The content of register SP is incremented by 2.

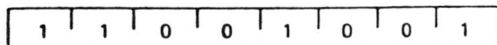

1	1	0	0	1	0	0	1

Cycles: 3

States: 10

Addressing: reg. indirect

Flags: none

Rcondition   (Conditional return)

If (CCC),

(PCL) ◄— ((SP))

(PCH) ◄— ((SP) + 1)

(SP) ◄— (SP) + 2

If the specified condition is true, the actions specified in the RET instruction (see above) are performed; otherwise, control continues sequentially.

1	1	C	C	C	0	0	0

Cycles: 1/3

States: 6/12

Addressing: reg. indirect

Flags: none

RST n   (Restart)

((SP) − 1) ◄— (PCH)

((SP) − 2) ◄— (PCL)

(SP) ◄— (SP) − 2

(PC) ◄— 8 · (NNN)

The high-order eight bits of the next instruction address are moved to the memory location whose address is one less than the content of register SP. The low-order eight bits of the next instruction address are moved to the memory location whose address is two less than the content of register SP. The content of register SP is decremented by two. Control is transferred to the instruction whose address is eight times the content of NNN.

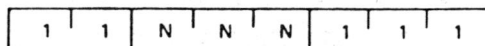

1	1	N	N	N	1	1	1

Cycles: 3

States: 12

Addressing: reg. indirect

Flags: none

15	14	13	12	11	10	9	8	7	6	5	4	3	2	1	0
0	0	0	0	0	0	0	0	0	0	N	N	N	0	0	0

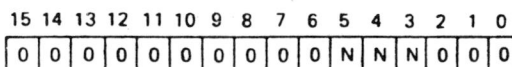

Program Counter After Restart

PCHL   (Jump H and L indirect — move H and L to PC)

(PCH) ◄— (H)

(PCL) ◄— (L)

The content of register H is moved to the high-order eight bits of register PC. The content of register L is moved to the low-order eight bits of register PC.

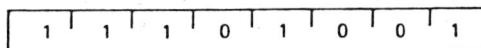

1	1	1	0	1	0	0	1

Cycles: 1

States: 6

Addressing: register

Flags: none

Stack, I/O, and Machine Control Group:

This group of instructions performs I/O, manipulates the Stack, and alters internal control flags.

Unless otherwise specified, condition flags are not affected by any instructions in this group.

FLAG WORD

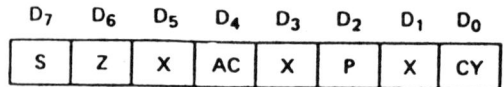

D_7	D_6	D_5	D_4	D_3	D_2	D_1	D_0
S	Z	X	AC	X	P	X	CY

X: undefined

PUSH rp   (Push)

$((SP) - 1) \leftarrow (rh)$

$((SP) - 2) \leftarrow (rl)$

$(SP) \leftarrow (SP) - 2$

The content of the high-order register of register pair rp is moved to the memory location whose address is one less than the content of register SP. The content of the low-order register of register pair rp is moved to the memory location whose address is two less than the content of register SP. The content of register SP is decremented by 2. Note: Register pair rp = SP may not be specified.

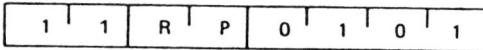

1	1	R	P	0	1	0	1

Cycles: 3
States: 12
Addressing: reg. indirect
Flags: none

PUSH PSW   (Push processor status word)

$((SP) - 1) \leftarrow (A)$

$((SP) - 2)_0 \leftarrow (CY) , ((SP) - 2)_1 \leftarrow 1$

$((SP) - 2)_2 \leftarrow (P) , ((SP) - 2)_3 \leftarrow 0$

$((SP) - 2)_4 \leftarrow (AC) , ((SP) - 2)_5 \leftarrow 0$

$((SP) - 2)_6 \leftarrow (Z) , ((SP) - 2)_7 \leftarrow (S)$

$(SP) \leftarrow (SP) - 2$

The content of register A is moved to the memory location whose address is one less than register SP. The contents of the condition flags are assembled into a processor status word and the word is moved to the memory location whose address is two less than the content of register SP. The content of register SP is decremented by two.

1	1	1	1	0	1	0	1

Cycles: 3
States: 12
Addressing: reg. indirect
Flags: none

POP rp   (Pop)

$(rl) \leftarrow ((SP))$

$(rh) \leftarrow ((SP) + 1)$

$(SP) \leftarrow (SP) + 2$

The content of the memory location, whose address is specified by the content of register SP, is moved to the low-order register of register pair rp. The content of the memory location, whose address is one more than the content of register SP, is moved to the high-order register of register pair rp. The content of register SP is incremented by 2. Note: Register pair rp = SP may not be specified.

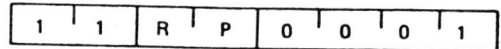

1	1	R	P	0	0	0	1

Cycles: 3
States: 10
Addressing: reg. indirect
Flags: none

POP PSW   (Pop processor status word)

$(CY) \leftarrow ((SP))_0$

$(P) \leftarrow ((SP))_2$

$(AC) \leftarrow ((SP))_4$

$(Z) \leftarrow ((SP))_6$

$(S) \leftarrow ((SP))_7$

$(A) \leftarrow ((SP) + 1)$

$(SP) \leftarrow (SP) + 2$

The content of the memory location whose address is specified by the content of register SP is used to restore the condition flags. The content of the memory location whose address is one more than the content of register SP is moved to register A. The content of register SP is incremented by 2.

1	1	1	1	0	0	0	1

Cycles: 3
States: 10
Addressing: reg. indirect
Flags: Z,S,P,CY,AC

XTHL   (Exchange stack top with H and L)

(L) ←→ ((SP))

(H) ←→ ((SP) + 1)

The content of the L register is exchanged with the content of the memory location whose address is specified by the content of register SP. The content of the H register is exchanged with the content of the memory location whose address is one more than the content of register SP.

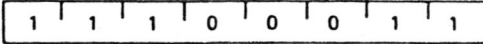

1	1	1	0	0	0	1	1

Cycles: 5
States: 16
Addressing: reg. indirect
Flags: none

SPHL   (Move HL to SP)

(SP) ←— (H) (L)

The contents of registers H and L (16 bits) are moved to register SP.

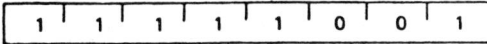

1	1	1	1	1	0	0	1

Cycles: 1
States: 6
Addressing: register
Flags: none

IN port   (Input)

(A) ←— (data)

The data placed on the eight bit bi-directional data bus by the specified port is moved to register A.

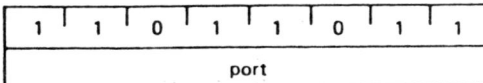

1	1	0	1	1	0	1	1
port							

Cycles: 3
States: 10
Addressing: direct
Flags: none

OUT port   (Output)

(data) ←— (A)

The content of register A is placed on the eight bit bi-directional data bus for transmission to the specified port.

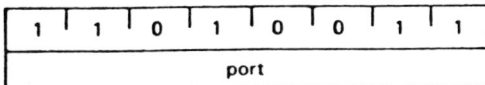

1	1	0	1	0	0	1	1
port							

Cycles: 3
States: 10
Addressing: direct
Flags: none

EI   (Enable interrupts)

The interrupt system is enabled following the execution of the next instruction.

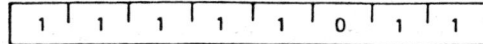

1	1	1	1	1	0	1	1

Cycles: 1
States: 4
Flags: none

DI   (Disable interrupts)

The interrupt system is disabled immediately following the execution of the DI instruction.

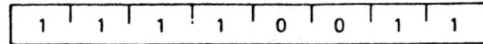

1	1	1	1	1	0	0	1	1

Cycles: 1
States: 4
Flags: none

HLT   (Halt)

The processor is stopped. The registers and flags are unaffected.

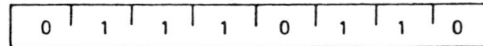

0	1	1	1	0	1	1	0

Cycles: 1
States: 5
Flags: none

NOP   (No op)

No operation is performed. The registers and flags are unaffected.

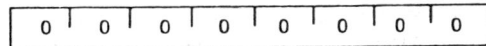

0	0	0	0	0	0	0	0

Cycles: 1
States: 4
Flags: none

RIM   (Read Interrupt Mask)

The accumulator is loaded with the restart interrupt masks, any pending interrupts, and the contents of the serial input data line (SID).

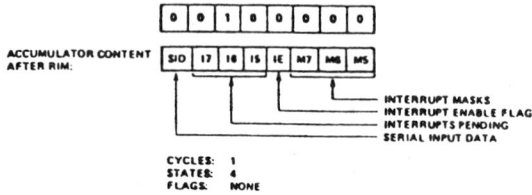

ACCUMULATOR CONTENT AFTER RIM:

| SID | I7 | I6 | I5 | IE | M7 | M6 | M5 |

INTERRUPT MASKS
INTERRUPT ENABLE FLAG
INTERRUPTS PENDING
SERIAL INPUT DATA

CYCLES: 1
STATES: 4
FLAGS: NONE

SIM   (Set Interrupt Masks)

The contents of the accumulator will be used in programming the restart interrupt masks. Bits 0–2 will set/reset the mask bit for RST 5.5, 6.5, 7.5 of the interrupt mask register, if bit 3 is 1 ("set"). Bit 3 is a "Mask Set Enable" control.

Setting the mask (i.e. masked bit = 1) disables the corresponding interrupt.

	Set	Reset
RST 5.5 MASK	if bit 0 = 1	if bit 0 = 0
RST 6.5 MASK	bit 1 = 1	bit 1 = 0
RST 7.5 MASK	bit 2 = 1	bit 2 = 0

RST 7.5, whether masked or not, will be reset if bit 4 = 1.

$\overline{\text{RESET IN}}$ input (pin 36) will set all RST MASKs, and reset/disable all interrupts.

SIM can, also, load the SOD output latch. Accumulator bit 7 is loaded into the SOD latch if bit 6 is set. The latch is unaffected if bit 6 is a zero. $\overline{\text{RESET IN}}$ input sets the SOD latch to zero.

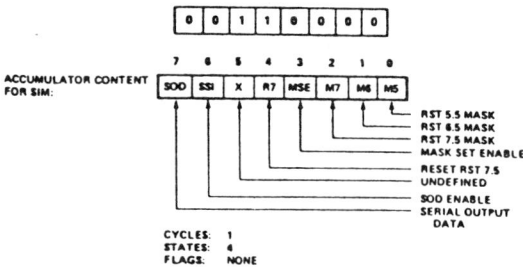

ACCUMULATOR CONTENT FOR SIM:

| 7 | 6 | 5 | 4 | 3 | 2 | 1 | 0 |
| SOD | SSE | X | R7 | MSE | M7 | M6 | M5 |

RST 5.5 MASK
RST 6.5 MASK
RST 7.5 MASK
MASK SET ENABLE
RESET RST 7.5
UNDEFINED
SOD ENABLE
SERIAL OUTPUT DATA

CYCLES: 1
STATES: 4
FLAGS: NONE

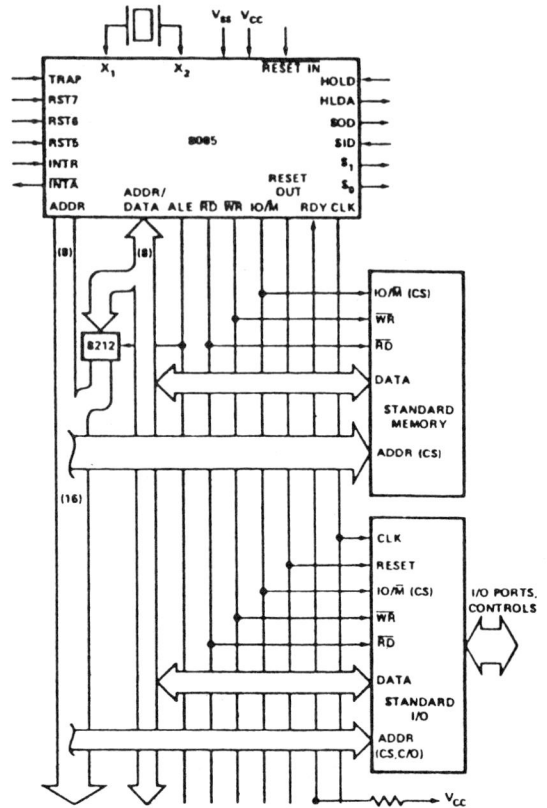

FIGURE 6. MCS-85™ MINIMUM SYSTEM (USING STANDARD MEMORIES).

Intel 8085A instruction set

Mnemonic	Description	Opcode (bits)							
		7	6	5	4	3	2	1	0

(a) *Move*
MOVE, LOAD, and STORE

Mnemonic	Description	7	6	5	4	3	2	1	0
MOV r1,r2	Move register 2 to register 1	0	1	D	D	D	S	S	S
MOV M,r	Move register to memory	0	1	1	1	0	S	S	S
MOV r,M	Move memory to register	0	1	D	D	D	1	1	0
MVI r	Move immediate	0	0	D	D	D	1	1	0
MVI M	Move immediate memory	0	0	1	1	0	1	1	0
LXI B	Load immediate register-pair B & C	0	0	0	0	0	0	0	1
LXI D	Load immediate register-pair D & E	0	0	0	1	0	0	0	1
LXI H	Load immediate register-pair H & L	0	0	1	0	0	0	0	1
LXI SP	Load immediate stack pointer	0	0	1	1	0	0	0	1
STAX B	Store A indirect (using B & C)	0	0	0	0	0	0	1	0
STAX D	Store A indirect (using D & E)	0	0	0	1	0	0	1	0
LDAX B	Load A indirect (using B & C)	0	0	0	0	1	0	1	0
LDAX D	Load A indirect (using D & E)	0	0	0	1	1	0	1	0
STA	Store A direct	0	0	1	1	0	0	1	0
LDA	Load A direct	0	0	1	1	1	0	1	0
SHLD	Store H & L direct	0	0	1	0	0	0	1	0
LHLD	Load H & L direct	0	0	1	0	1	0	1	0
XCHG	Exchange D & E and H & L registers	1	1	1	0	1	0	1	1

INPUT/OUTPUT

Mnemonic	Description	7	6	5	4	3	2	1	0
IN	Input	1	1	0	1	1	0	1	1
OUT	Output	1	1	0	1	0	0	1	1

(b) *Modify*
INCREMENT and DECREMENT

Mnemonic	Description	7	6	5	4	3	2	1	0
INR r	Increment register	0	0	D	D	D	1	0	0
DCR r	Decrement register	0	0	D	D	D	1	0	1
INR M	Increment memory	0	0	1	1	0	1	0	0
DCR M	Decrement memory	0	0	1	1	0	1	0	1
INX B	Increment B & C registers	0	0	0	0	0	0	1	1
INX D	Increment D & E registers	0	0	0	1	0	0	1	1
INX H	Increment H & L registers	0	0	1	0	0	0	1	1
INX SP	Increment stack pointer	0	0	1	1	0	0	1	1
DCX B	Decrement B & C	0	0	0	0	1	0	1	1
DCX D	Decrement D & E	0	0	0	1	1	0	1	1
DCX H	Decrement H & L	0	0	1	0	1	0	1	1
DCX SP	Decrement stack pointer	0	0	1	1	1	0	1	1

continued over

Intel 8085A instruction set – *continued*

Mnemonic	Description	Opcode (bits)							
		7	6	5	4	3	2	1	0
ADD									
ADD r	Add register to A	1	0	0	0	0	S	S	S
ADC r	Add register to A with carry	1	0	0	0	1	S	S	S
ADD M	Add memory to A	1	0	0	0	0	1	1	0
ADC M	Add memory to A with carry	1	0	0	0	1	1	1	0
ADI	Add immediate to A	1	1	0	0	0	1	1	0
ACI	Add immediate to A with carry	1	1	0	0	1	1	1	0
DAD B	Add B & C to H & L	0	0	0	0	1	0	0	1
DAD D	Add D & E to H & L	0	0	0	1	1	0	0	1
DAD H	Add H & L to H & L	0	0	1	0	1	0	0	1
DAD SP	Add stack pointer to H & L	0	0	1	1	1	0	0	1
SUBTRACT									
SUB r	Subtract register from A	1	0	0	1	0	S	S	S
SBB r	Subtract register from A with borrow	1	0	0	1	1	S	S	S
SUB M	Subtract memory from A	1	0	0	1	0	1	1	0
SBB M	Subtract memory from A with borrow	1	0	0	1	1	1	1	0
SUI	Subtract immediate from A	1	1	0	1	0	1	1	0
SBI	Subtract immediate from A with borrow	1	1	0	1	1	1	1	0
LOGICAL									
ANA r	AND register with A	1	0	1	0	0	S	S	S
XRA r	EXCLUSIVE OR register with A	1	0	1	0	1	S	S	S
ORA r	OR register with A	1	0	1	1	0	S	S	S
CMP r	Compare register with A	1	0	1	1	1	S	S	S
ANA M	AND memory with A	1	0	1	0	0	1	1	0
XRA M	EXCLUSIVE OR memory with A	1	0	1	0	1	1	1	0
ORA M	OR memory with A	1	0	1	1	0	1	1	0
CMP M	Compare memory with A	1	0	1	1	1	1	1	0
ANI	AND immediate with A	1	1	1	0	0	1	1	0
XRI	EXCLUSIVE OR immediate with A	1	1	1	0	1	1	1	0
ORI	OR immediate with A	1	1	1	1	0	1	1	0
CPI	Compare immediate with A	1	1	1	1	1	1	1	0
ROTATE									
RLC	Rotate A left	0	0	0	0	0	1	1	1
RRC	Rotate A right	0	0	0	0	1	1	1	1
RAL	Rotate A left through carry	0	0	0	1	0	1	1	1
RAR	Rotate A right through carry	0	0	0	1	1	1	1	1

Mnemonic	Description	Opcode (bits)							
		7	6	5	4	3	2	1	0

SPECIALS

Mnemonic	Description	7	6	5	4	3	2	1	0
CMA	Complement A	0	0	1	0	1	1	1	1
STC	Set carry	0	0	1	1	0	1	1	1
CMC	Complement carry	0	0	1	1	1	1	1	1
DAA	Decimal adjust A	0	0	1	0	0	1	1	1

(c) *Jump*

JUMP

Mnemonic	Description	7	6	5	4	3	2	1	0
JMP	Jump unconditional	1	1	0	0	0	0	1	1
JC	Jump on carry	1	1	0	1	1	0	1	0
JNC	Jump on no carry	1	1	0	1	0	0	1	0
JZ	Jump on zero	1	1	0	0	1	0	1	0
JNZ	Jump on no zero	1	1	0	0	0	0	1	0
JP	Jump on positive	1	1	1	1	0	0	1	0
JM	Jump on minus	1	1	1	1	1	0	1	0
JPE	Jump on parity even	1	1	1	0	1	0	1	0
JPO	Jump on parity odd	1	1	1	0	0	0	1	0
PCHL	H & L to program counter	1	1	1	0	1	0	0	1

(d) *Subroutine*

CALL

Mnemonic	Description	7	6	5	4	3	2	1	0
CALL	Call unconditional	1	1	0	0	1	1	0	1
CC	Call on carry	1	1	0	1	1	1	0	0
CNC	Call on no carry	1	1	0	1	0	1	0	0
CZ	Call on zero	1	1	0	0	1	1	0	0
CNZ	Call on no zero	1	1	0	0	0	1	0	0
CP	Call on positive	1	1	1	1	0	1	0	0
CM	Call on minus	1	1	1	1	1	1	0	0
CPE	Call on parity even	1	1	1	0	1	1	0	0
CPO	Call on parity odd	1	1	1	0	0	1	0	0

RETURN

Mnemonic	Description	7	6	5	4	3	2	1	0
RET	Return	1	1	0	0	1	0	0	1
RC	Return on carry	1	1	0	1	1	0	0	0
RNC	Return on no carry	1	1	0	1	0	0	0	0
RZ	Return on zero	1	1	0	0	1	0	0	0
RNZ	Return on no zero	1	1	0	0	0	0	0	0
RP	Return on positive	1	1	1	1	0	0	0	0
RM	Return on minus	1	1	1	1	1	0	0	0
RPE	Return on parity even	1	1	1	0	1	0	0	0
RPO	Return on parity odd	1	1	1	0	0	0	0	0

continued over

Intel 8085A instruction set — *continued*

Mnemonic	Description	Opcode (bits)							
		7	6	5	4	3	2	1	0

(e) *Stack*

STACK

Mnemonic	Description	7	6	5	4	3	2	1	0
PUSH B	Push register-pair B & C on stack	1	1	0	0	0	1	0	1
PUSH D	Push register-pair D & E on stack	1	1	0	1	0	1	0	1
PUSH H	Push register-pair H & L on stack	1	1	1	0	0	1	0	1
PUSH PSW	Push A and flags on stack	1	1	1	1	0	1	0	1
POP B	Pop register-pair B & C off stack	1	1	0	0	0	0	0	1
POP D	Pop register-pair D & E off stack	1	1	0	1	0	0	0	1
POP H	Pop register-pair H & L off stack	1	1	1	0	0	0	0	1
POP PSW	Pop A and flags off stack	1	1	1	1	0	0	0	1
XTHL	Exchange top of stack and H & L	1	1	1	0	0	0	1	1
SPHL	H & L to stack pointer	1	1	1	1	1	0	0	1

(f) *Interrupts and control*

INTERRUPTS

Mnemonic	Description	7	6	5	4	3	2	1	0
EI	Enable interrupts	1	1	1	1	1	0	1	1
DI	Disable interrupts	1	1	1	1	0	0	1	1
RIM	Read interrupt mask	0	0	1	0	0	0	0	0
SIM	Set interrupt mask	0	0	1	1	0	0	0	0

CONTROL

Mnemonic	Description	7	6	5	4	3	2	1	0
NOP	No-operation	0	0	0	0	0	0	0	0
HLT	Halt	0	1	1	1	0	1	1	0
RST	Restart	1	1	A	A	A	1	1	1

DDD or SSS   B — 000; C — 001; D — 010; E — 011; H — 100; L — 101
         Memory — 110; A — 111

Answers to Exercises

Chapter 1

Section 1.1

1. CPU, memory, input/output

2. Printer, floppy disk, keyboard, CRT

3. The busses are the three parallel wire inter-connection highways which link the CPU to memory and input/output devices. They are the address, data, and control busses.

4. (a) 8   (b) 16

5. The crystal regulates the CPU clock to a precise frequency.

6. 1M byte

8. Read/Write

9. CPU, ROM, RAM, input/output, address decoder

10. CPU — in fact it is the Zilog Z80 microprocessor

11. The following pin functions are required:
    - (a) Address bus — 16
    - (b) Data bus   — 8
    - (c) D.C. power — 4
    - (d) Crystal   — 2   (or crystal
                  —   oscillator circuit)
            Total = 30

    Therefore 10 (40−30) pins are available for control lines, assuming the standard 40-pin package.

12. The pin functions of a 1024×8 ROM are:
    - (a) Address lines — 10   ($2^{10} = 1024$)
    - (b) Data lines   — 8

    - (c) Chip Select   — 1
    - (d) D.C. power   — 2

13. The pin functions of a 256×8 RAM are:
    - (a) Address lines — 8   ($2^8 = 256$)
    - (b) Data lines   —8
    - (c) Write Enable — 1   (WE)
    - (d) Chip Select   —1
    - (e) D.C. power   —2

16. (a) ROM

    (b) The pin functions are:

Address lines (A0 to A11)	— 12	($2^{12} = 4096$ locations)
Data lines D0 to D7	— 8	(read only)
Chip Select (CS1 and CS2)	— 2	(both Chip Select signals must be active for a read operation)
D.C. power (V_{CC} and V_{SS})	— 2	(single power supply)

Section 1.2

17. The implementation of each instruction comprises the fetch/execute cycle. The fetch operation involves a memory read operation, i.e., the opcode is read from memory into the CPUs instruction register.

18. The crossover effect denotes the fact that the signal can go high (logic 1) or low (logic 0).

19. It is better if a microprocessor contains its own oscillator (or multivibrator) circuit so that a saving in external circuitry can be made.

20. Instruction (a) is approximately three times faster than (b). Instruction (b) requires three memory read operations in place of one.

21. No

22. Yes

23. As for Example 21, with 12 address lines (A0 to A11) connected to RAM

24. (a) Address lines are not allowed sufficient time to settle before data lines are reset.
    (b) Write pulse occurs after data lines are reset.

25. As for Example 22, with additional control signals READ and IOS connected

Chapter 2

Section 2.1

1. (d), (b), (a), (c)

2. 40

3. Software polling

4. The program attempts to output the second character immediately after the first character. The printer will not have finished processing the first character, and so either a program delay or a check on printer busy is required between the two output operations.

5. The 'status' of a peripheral device is an indication of whether or not it is busy processing a data item.

6. The interrupt signal causes suspension of the main program and immediate entry into an interrupt routine which can service the interrupt.

7. 'Initializing' a programmable input/output IC is setting its ports to be input or output.

8. (c)

9. POLL : IN   21H
         JNZ   POLL
         MVI   A,00H
         OUT   20H

10. Handshaking is the method of requesting data transfer by setting a signal in one direction and authorizing that transfer by a signal in the reverse direction.

11. Use interrupt driven system. This gives an immediate response. Polling the alarm contact, after completing scanning and processing the A/D converters readings, will give a slow response to a change of state of that contact.

12. Control bus.

13. Save contents of program counter and work registers.

15. Time delay loop.

16. Program operation is suspended.

17. (a) Fast data transfer without the need for a program to implement the transfer.
    (b) Extra circuitry.

Section 2.2

18. An input/output port is an eight-bit parallel input/output channel which is connected to a microcomputer via an input/output interface device.

19. Status signals are input signals from a peripheral and represent the state (e.g., busy) of the peripheral.

20. A latched output bit is a signal which is staticized, i.e., once set it will not alter unless changed by a subsequent output operation.

21. A 'control register' is simply an address on a programmable input/output IC to which control data are sent by software in order to initialize the ports as input or output. Similarly, the 'control register' of a UART is used to initialize the baud rate, etc.

22. Parallel.

23. Insufficient pins—two ports require 16 pins, plus address, control, and data bus requirements.

26. Hex. 38, i.e., 00111000.

27. Universal asynchronous receiver transmitter.

28. A shift register converts parallel to serial data, or vice versa.

29. 480.

31. (a) Serial, to save cable costs (two wires in place of perhaps nine).
    (b) Parallel, to give fast data transfer (the fastest baud rates from most UARTs are 2400 or 4800).

32. START : IN   00H
              RLC
              OUT   01H

33. (a) Voltage levels should be:
        logic $1 = -9$ V approximately
        logic $0 = +9$ V approximately
    (b) There cannot be nine data bits—seven is normal.
    (c) Stop bit should be a logic 1.

34. HOLD and HOLDA.

35. Use two 8-bit tristate latches, e.g., 74LS373.

36. To save software overhead of scanning keyboard; the keyboard encoder IC performs this function by hardware.

37. To frame the serial bits read via the head from the disk surface on the Read Data line.

38. The Head Load signal causes the head to be placed in contact with the disk surface.

Chapter 3

Section 3.1

1. CALL.

2. All are true except (b). Statement (d) is true because the CALL and RET instructions are additional.

3. The return address must be staticized to enable the main program to be re-entered.

4. A return instruction does not contain an address. The return location could be anywhere in the main program; it is the address of the instruction which follows the CALL instruction.

5. The program loops continuously from the subroutine back to TOM; it does not return to CHARLIE to allow the program to proceed. Also the program is badly structured—the subroutine should be segregated away from the main program.

6. (b).

7. (a) Main program:
```
MVI   A,40H
STA   1000H
CALL  SUB
```
   (b) Subroutine:
```
SUB : LDA   1000H
      CPI   40H
      JNZ   SKIP
      MVI   A,1
      OUT   01H
SKIP : RET
```

8.

	MVI C,0	Zero highest value
	MVI B,10	Number of data values
	LXI H,1000H	Start address of data values
SEARCH:	MOV A, M	Load data value
	CMP C	Compare with highest value
	JNC LOW	Jump if less
	MOV C,A	Overwrite highest value
LOW:	INX H	Next data value
	DCR B	Decrement loop count
	JNZ SEARCH	Repeat 10 times
	RET	Return to main program

Section 3.2

9. A nested subroutine is a subroutine which is called by another subroutine.

10. The return address is stored on the stack *automatically* when the CALL instruction is obeyed.

11. The only limit to stack size is the end of RAM memory—the stack expands towards the lowest addresses.

12. Memory (RAM).

13. Stack pointer. 16 bits.

14. The stack commences at memory address 0000, i.e., the first location in memory. Therefore the stack cannot be used because it requires to expand backwards through memory.

15. The use of the PUSH instruction within the subroutine displaces the stack pointer so that the return instruction will be unsuccessful.

16. Stack pointer = 001E, contents = 80 hex.

17. PUSH B
PUSH D
Therefore eight bytes are saved.

18. The stack *can* handle this arrangement, and the maximum usage of the stack in this arrangement is six bytes.

19. (a) On the stack, (b) in CPU registers, (c) in memory locations.

Chapter 4

Section 4.1

1. An interrupt signal is an external signal which when set interrupts the execution of the current program.

2. A subroutine is software activated (CALL instruction); an interrupt routine is hardware activated (by an external signal).

3. (a) Interrupt, (b) polling, (c) interrupt.

4. A nested interrupt is an interrupt which interrupts another interrupt routine.

5. Highest priority first: (b), (c), (a), (d).

6. A power-up interrupt is applied to a micro-computer after a short delay when the machine is switched on to allow time for the d.c. power supplies to settle.

7. An individual interrupt can be blocked by setting the appropriate bit in the interrupt mask.

8. $a = 3$, $b = 2$, $c = 2$, $d = 1$, $e = 1$, $f = 3$, $g = 3$.

9. A timer interrupt can be used by software to maintain a time-of-day clock count in memory. Also regular scans of external signals can be initiated by the timer interrupt routine.

10. (a) Power-down (highest priority)
(b) Interval timer
(c) Weight signal ready.

11. Unused interrupts are often masked to prevent spurious operation.

Section 4.2

12. An interrupt vector indicates the start address of an interrupt routine.

13. (a) Jump to an address.
(b) Address only (jump is inferred).

14. The registers cannot be pushed onto the stack in a main program prior to an interrupt because the precise occurrence of the interrupt cannot be estimated.

15. The EI function enables the whole interrupt system.

16. Yes.

17.
003C	*0200*
(*interrupt vector*)	(*interrupt routine*)
JMP 0200H	PUSH PSW
	LDA 1000H
	INR A
	STA 1000H
	POP PSW
	EI
	RET

0300
(*main program*)
```
START : MVI   A,1
        OUT   02H
        CALL  DELAY
        MVI   A,0
        OUT   02H
        CALL  DELAY
        JMP   START
```

18. (a) No.
    (b) Yes—the execution time of the interrupt routine adds to the time of the delay section.

19. Yes—TRAP is the highest priority interrupt and cannot be masked.

20. (a) RST 7.5 and RST 5.5.
    (b) RST 5.5 only.

21. The interrupt vector area is ROM-based and so additional vectors cannot be included.

Chapter 5

Section 5.1

1. (a) ROM, PROM, EPROM.
   (b) Static RAM, dynamic RAM.

2. Interconnection signals (e.g., outputs) possess electrical characteristics which enable connection to TTL circuits; the most important electrical characteristic is $+5\,V$ and $0\,V$ signal levels.

3. Ten address lines, eight data lines, one chip select, two d.c. power supply.

4. 16K (2048×8) EPROM.

5. Reinstating stored bits (faster than once every 2 ms) to prevent data loss—performed by setting the least significant half of the address lines.

6. MOS.

7. 500 ns.

8. The bar indicates that inverse logic is used, i.e., the signal is set (the chip is selected) when the signal is at logic 0.

9. (a) By exposure to UV light.
   (b) All bits are set to 1 after erasure.
   (c) The erasure window should be covered with an opaque label after programming in order to prevent accidental erasure.

10. An eight-bit microprocessor possesses 16 address lines which give a total addressing range of 64K. Thus only one half of a 128K chip can be accessed.

11. Nibble storage is storage in four-bit modules, e.g., four-bit static RAM devices.

12. The two signals must be combined in an additional circuit outside the chip before connection is made to the bidirectional data bus.

13. RAM is required for: (a) stack, (b) temporary storage of plant data.

14. RAM, 1K (256×4).

15. 2708 is 8K (1024×8) EPROM, cf. 2716 which is 16K (2048×8) EPROM.

16. A program can be tested and prototyped on a 2716 EPROM, and then transferred to a 2316 ROM for volume production in order to reduce cost.

17. Cheaper, smaller, lower power, faster.

18. ROM.

19. The address lines are presented to the IC on a time-multiplexed basis. The least significant half is first set together with the Row Select signal; the most significant half is then set together with the Column Select signal.
Advantage: reduces number of pins, and therefore the size of the IC.

20. Last line:

    6p   25p   60p   37p

Section 5.2

21. Decoder or address decoder.

22. 110 (bottom input first).

23. A bus driver increases the drive capability of an address, data, or control bus line.

25. 3 to 8 decoder.

26. (a) 0800,   (b) 0400,   (c) 0000 and 0001

27. Start address = 2800
    End address = 2BFF

28. An 8K ROM chip requires 13 address lines (A0 to A12) to select each memory location in the device. However, the circuit in Example 5 uses A12 for address decoding. A12 cannot be used for both purposes.

29. RAM1 and RAM2 should share the same Chip Select signal since they are four-bit devices and store different halves of the same memory byte.

32. (a) Chips 1, 2, 3, and 4 are 256×4 RAM.
    Chips 5 and 6 are 4096×8 ROM.
    Chips 7 and 8 are 2 to 4 decoders.
  (b) Chips 1 and 2 have base address 0000.
    Chips 3 and 4 have base address 0100.
    Chip 5 has base address 1000.
    Chip 6 has base address 3000.

(c) A0 to A10, D0 to D7, SPARE4 (chip select for additional ROM).

(d) The NOR gate is necessary to prevent the Chip Select signals for chips 1 to 4 being set when chips 5 and 6 are addressed, i.e., to prevent selection of RAM when ROM is addressed.

Chapter 6

1. (a) Interval timer to generate single time delay.
  (b) Continuous pulses, which are normally on interrupt, to give a real-time clock.
  (c) Event counter to count external pulses.

2. (a) Software polling, (b) interrupt.

3. An interval timer produces a precise time delay and the main program can perform other software functions during the delay period.

4. The CPU clock is used to decrement the interval timer counter.

5. The counter-timer is set to the increment mode when it is required to count external pulses/events.

6. Setting an interval timer requires the setting of the eight-bit lower order half of the count, the higher order half, and the control register.

7. Possible uses of a 10 ms interrupt:
  (a) trigger regular software tasks, e.g., scan keyboard;
  (b) maintain time-of-day clock for reporting on printer and VDU, and also to trigger time-dependent events.

8. Hex. 2710 (= decimal 10000).

9. (a) CPU clock ϕ
  (b) Real-time clock from counter-timer chip.

11. (a) Connect A0 to A_n.
  (b) Connect A1 to A_{n+1}.

(c) Connect A4 and A5 to a 2 to 4 decoder; third output from decoder is fed to CS.

Chapter 7

1. Machine code is the binary (or hex. equivalent) code for program instructions which is loaded into memory and is executed when the program is run.

2. BASIC, PASCAL, FORTRAN (also COBOL, ALGOL, etc.).

3. A pseudo-instruction is a non-executable command to the assembler.

4. (a) Use mnemonics in place of opcode hex. or binary.
   (b) Use labels in place of absolute memory addresses.

5. Monitor.

6. (a) A program breakpoint is a location at which program execution is stopped, so that debugging can occur, e.g., by examination of contents of registers and memory locations.
   (b) A single-shot operation is a debugging program facility which executes one instruction only of the program under test.

7. (a) Assembler, (b) debugging program.